The Blood-Stained Poppy

The Blood-Stained Poppy

Kevin Rooney & James Heartfield

Winchester, UK
Washington, USA

JOHN HUNT PUBLISHING

First published by Zero Books, 2019
Zero Books is an imprint of John Hunt Publishing Ltd., No. 3 East St., Alresford,
Hampshire SO24 9EE, UK
office@jhpbooks.com
www.johnhuntpublishing.com
www.zero-books.net

For distributor details and how to order please visit the 'Ordering' section on our website.

Design: Stuart Davies

UK: Printed and bound by CPI Group (UK) Ltd, Croydon, CR0 4YY
US: Printed and bound by Thomson-Shore, 7300 West Joy Road, Dexter, MI 48130

Contents

Also by the Authors

Who's Afraid of the Easter Rising?, Zero Books, 2015

Introduction

At half-time during a football game at Celtic Park in 2010, a group of Celtic supporters unfurled a banner which read:

> Your deeds they would shame all the devils in hell. Ireland, Iraq, Afghanistan. No blood-stained poppy on our hoops.

It was a protest against the club's decision to mark Remembrance Day by getting the players to wear red poppies on their famous green and white jerseys and observe a minute's silence before the game. Anyone who knows the history and traditions of Celtic Football Club would not have been too surprised to see a group of fans unfurling an anti-war banner. A significant section of the support would self-identify as left-wing and anti-imperialist. A significant section would be sympathetic to Irish republicanism and other similar causes like expressing solidarity with the Palestinians. None of this is new. These fans have a long record of voicing opposition to what they see as British militarism. Expecting every Celtic supporter to accept without protest the implanting of the Earl Haig poppy onto the club jersey was never going to happen.

It was a remarkable demonisation of people for staging a peaceful protest. John Reid, club chairman and former Labour Home Secretary, pledged to 'hunt down' this 'hate-mob' and ban them from Celtic Park for life. One MP argued that the club needed to go further to 'lance this boil'. 'Celtic Shame', 'yobs' and 'louts' were typical newspaper headlines reporting the protest. There were calls for the police to arrest the perpetrators. The police duly promised to 'track these people down'. In the years since, Celtic fans have been threatened with arrest for declining to observe the Remembrance Day minute's silence before matches.[1]

If refusing to accept the imposition of a 'minute's silence' to honour soldiers who fought in wars you disagree with can get you arrested, then it is time to speak out. Britain is becoming a very intolerant society where basic civil liberties can no longer be taken for granted. In recent years a culture of conformism surrounding the politics of military remembrance has emerged where to question anything about it is to be judged deviant and beyond the pale.

Celtic fans protest against the poppy

Not every example of poppymania is so sharply contested. In 2014 artist Paul Cummins planted 888,246 ceramic poppies, one for each of the British and colonial war dead, in the moat of the Tower of London. It was an impressive field of red that moved many. The art worked because of the sheer number of poppies, and our knowing that each one was a life lost. But that is to make us think about the great sorrow of so many lives lost, without thinking about why. In official commemorations sadness for the soldiers killed is turned into a worship of the military institutions that sacrificed them. War memorials then and now take an emotional charge from the war dead. But they also turn the misery of war into a sanctification of the armies that made those wars.

In years gone by anti-war campaigners challenged the red poppy with a pacifist white poppy. If you really cared about the dead, the white poppy wearers said, you would fight against war. The Haig Fund (now the Royal British Legion's Poppy Appeal) poppy sellers reacted angrily to the Peace Pledge Union's white poppy when it first appeared.

Nowadays there are other variations on the poppy theme. But their point is not to challenge the militarism implicit in the poppy appeal. Rather they are hoping to be recognised for the part they played in the war. There are black poppy badges to honour the West Indian and African regiments that fought in the Great War. The loyalists of Northern Ireland have badges that combine the poppy with the red hand of Ulster. Ireland's Taoiseach has popularised the 'Shamrock Poppy', for the Irish who served in the British Army. There was even a purple poppy to recognise the animals that were killed in the war. 'Me too' these badges say: 'I want to be included in the war dead'. But we say that it is better that there should not be any more war dead.

Each year, the expectation to conform to poppymania grows. The sentimentalisation of areas of everyday life previously untouched by the politics of remembrance grows every year. Those who refuse to join in honouring British military dead are met with reprimands and restrictions. By all means let those who wish to honour the British military dead do so but let us defend the right of others to refuse. It is not only a problem of intolerance towards those who conscientiously object to the red poppy that needs to be challenged but also the unquestioning reverence with which everyone is now expected to treat the politics of the remembrance season.

In a climate where it has become more increasingly difficult to dispute the politics of official remembrance, there is a danger of historical amnesia setting in; it seems few really do 'remember' why so many people died in Britain's wars. We contend they rarely died for freedom. For the most part, they lost their lives in the service of British colonialism, Empire and the pursuit of reactionary ends. From Kenya to Malaysia, Cyprus to Iraq, the history of British militarism is shameful. That is why, once upon a time, there were many principled anti-imperialists in Britain and Ireland who stood up not only against war but also the red poppy and what it represented. Today unfortunately they are much fewer in number. Opposition leader Jeremy Corbyn once chose not to wear the poppy. For that he was attacked in the Press. After a heap of political and media pressure he now stands with the political and military elite at the Cenotaph in November with his head bowed. Who now will challenge the political and military elite who stand at Whitehall on 11 November?

Who will challenge the legitimacy of these decision makers responsible for unnecessary wars which sent people out to kill and be killed? This book intends to take up that baton. We stand full square in the anti-war camp and contend that to be anti-war means challenging the politics of official remembrance. It also requires a critique of the political and military leaders who stood at the Cenotaph in the past 100 years because they are largely culpable for the conflicts Britain has been involved in since the First World War. And did it help Jeremy Corbyn to go to the Cenotaph? No. He was criticised for 'not bowing deep enough'.

In the chapters that follow, we lay out the case for rejecting the red poppy and official remembrance. Let us briefly outline the thinking behind our approach. November 2018 marked the centenary of the end of the First World War. Since 2014 the start of the war, the centenaries of various battles fought have been marked by official remembrance and mass displays of the poppy in attempts to unify public sentiment in commemorating this conflict in which 20 million people died. The dominant narrative is that 100 years ago, we were all in it together so today we should remember together. The official commemorations have been led by the Royal family, military leaders and government politicians. Speaking at a press conference to launch the 1914-18 centenary commemoration and pledge £55 million, then Conservative Prime Minister David Cameron stated that the aim was to celebrate 'Britishness' and what he calls 'our national spirit'. Shortly after, the then Education Secretary, Michael Gove told us that the British went to war in 1914 to defend democracy and 'the western liberal order'. Several times during the centenary events, he highlighted the dangers of left-wing teachers, academics and others denigrating 'patriotism, honour and courage', insisting that Britain's role in the world reflects its 'special tradition of liberty'. The military historian Max Hastings told us that the war poets' view of the First World War was false, and that Britain was fighting for the freedom of Europe.

This book aims to challenge the narrative that we commemorate together and wear the poppy with pride. We contend that this war was an imperialist bloodbath which sent millions of mostly working-class men to their deaths. It is worth recalling the words of the last surviving veteran of the First World War, Harry Patch, who died in 2009:

> War is organised murder, nothing else...politicians who took us to war should have been given the guns and told to settle their differences themselves, instead of organising nothing better than legalised mass murder.

When it comes to marking the centenary of the end of the First World War and moving forward, we think it is time for open-minded citizens to step forward and question the propaganda and dull conformism of the red poppy and remembrance. Rather than expressions of sorrow or pride, let us embrace the restlessness of our anger and reject the official war commemorations and the poppy as blood-stained symbols of British militarism. Millions upon millions of human beings slaughtered and maimed in the service of what? Not for democracy, not for freedom, not any remotely progressive cause whatsoever. The lesson of the First World War is that imperialism and militarism, be it in its British, French or German guise, leads to human catastrophe and should be rejected. As Harry Patch asked:

> Why should the British government call me up and take me out to a battlefield to shoot a man I never knew, whose language I couldn't speak? All those lives lost for a war finished over a table. Now what is the sense in that?

The carnage at the Somme and at Passchendaele was not a struggle between good and evil, or a 'necessary sacrifice', as certain revisionist historians would have us believe. Rather, it was a struggle between evil and evil, and an utter waste of life. Failure to successfully challenge the slaughter of the First World War allowed the British military to spend much of the following century engaged in violent colonial adventures in every corner of the world.

A variant of the Great War narrative is that it was a case of 'lions led by donkeys'. The image is of an elitist class-ridden British military who were incompetent, cold hearted and who made profoundly stupid tactical decisions on the battlefield leading to unnecessarily high casualty figures. General Douglas Haig's dubious decision to repeatedly order hopeless attacks on the Somme is a case in point. Up to 20,000 men a day would die in this horrific battlefront alone due to Haig's military decisions. The 'lions led by donkeys' account is popularised in literature and is a common theme in school assemblies across Britain, every November. The problem is that this oversimplified image, while having some truth in it, serves as a distraction and allows British imperialism off the hook. As the socialist, historian and anti-war campaigner Neil Faulkner put it:

> The real criticism of men like Douglas Haig, the British commander-in-chief on the Western Front, is not that he was a 'donkey'. It was that he was a leading member of a rapacious ruling class, prepared to sacrifice millions of ordinary men in a war for empire and profit.[2]

Put bluntly, the real indictment of the battles of the Somme and Passchendaele is not tactical mistakes or that they were misconceived or mismanaged, though they absolutely were. It is that they were ever fought at all. For us in November 2018, the centenary of the end of the First World War is not only an opportunity to put up a criticism of imperialism – the cause of the war – but also to challenge the politics of commemoration surrounding it. In essence the book is a critique of Britain's military wars, it is even more so a challenge to how we are being asked to remember them. Our starting point is that we have nothing in common with those in the British ruling class who since the First World War have launched countless other bloody conflicts. We stand in opposition to militarism. We genuinely sympathise with the relatives of British soldiers who have died needlessly in these conflicts. It is because we do care that we wish to challenge the often-dishonest way that the red poppy and remembrance are used not to promote genuine peace but instead to turn grief into legitimacy for militarism.

Chapter One

Origins of the Red Poppy

In New York, on Saturday 9 November 1918, just two days before the Armistice that ended the First World War, Moina Michael lifted up a copy of a journal recently placed on her desk by a young soldier. As she began to read, she came across a marked page which carried Colonel John McCrae's poem *We Shall Not Sleep*, later named *In Flanders Fields*. She had read the poem many times before but this time, the last verse transfixed her:

> To you from failing hands we throw the Torch; be yours to hold it high. If ye break faith with us who die, we shall not sleep, though poppies grow in Flanders Fields.

In her book, *The Miracle Flower: The Story of the Flanders Fields Memorial Poppy*, Moina Michael described reading the last verse of McCrae's poem as a profound experience. Reflecting upon the countless thousands of allied soldiers who had lost their lives in the trenches of Flanders and elsewhere, she pondered on the words of the poem.

> *To you from failing hands we throw*
> *The torch; be yours to hold it high.*
> *If ye break faith with us who die*
> *We shall not sleep*

Michael continued:

> This was for me a full spiritual experience. It seemed as though the silent voices again were vocal, whispering in sighs of anxiety unto anguish.

Prompted by these words which deeply affected her, she determined that the deaths of these soldiers would not be forgotten. She decided to act.

> Alone again, in a high moment of white resolve, I pledged to keep the faith and always to wear a red poppy of Flanders Fields as a sign of remembrance and the emblem of keeping faith with all who died.

This was the moment that gave birth to the red remembrance poppy as we know it today. Over the coming weeks and months, this teacher, Christian and supporter of the allied cause embarked on a campaign to promote the wearing of the red poppy on Armistice Day in memory of those allied soldiers who died during the Great War. So successful was her campaign to persuade numerous organisations to adopt this red emblem, that Michael soon became known as the 'Poppy Lady'.[1]

Swept by a tide of emotion provoked by McCrae's *In Flanders Fields* poem she wrote her own poetic tribute to the allied dead:

> *Oh! You who sleep in Flanders' fields,*
> *Sleep sweet – to rise anew!*
> *We caught the torch you threw,*
> *And holding high we keep the faith*
> *With all who died.*
> *We cherish too, the poppy red,*
> *That grows on fields where valour led.*
> *It seems to signal to the skies*
> *That blood of heroes never dies,*
> *But lends a lustre to the red*
> *Of the flower that blooms above the dead*
> *In Flanders' fields.*
> *And now the torch and Poppy Red*
> *We wear in honour of the dead.*

Fear not that ye have died for naught
We'll teach the lesson that ye taught
In Flanders' fields.

Her words captured the spirit of the time among many like her who had supported the war. She hoped that the words would ease the conscience of so many who were wondering why the war had been fought and why so many young men had died. She travelled across North America promoting the red poppy to be adopted as the official symbol of war remembrance. As US soldiers began returning home from the war in Europe in 1919, some of the home coming events began to be decorated with the red paper poppies. By 1920, delegates at the American Legion's national convention passed a resolution to champion the poppy's cause.

Among the visitors to that 1920 convention was a well-connected French widow named Anna E. Guerin. Within a short period of time, Guerin would help export the poppy emblem around the world. She shared Michael's passion for the poppy as a symbol of remembrance. Guerin would mass produce the poppy across all the allied nations of the world and they would reach millions of people. In August 1921, she travelled to London to show a sample of her poppies to the newly founded British Legion. Douglas Haig, who had been Britain's senior military commander during the war and led the forces at the Battle of the Somme, liked her proposal and so the British Legion adopted it as part of its appeal fund.[2] Nine million poppies were ordered for the first Poppy Day to be held in Britain on the 11 November and the rest, as they say, is history.

The standard interpretation is that the poppy is an apolitical symbol. It is and should be above politics, we are told. It is little more than an ethical duty to the dead. Wrapped up in the imagery of poppy remembrance is the sacrifice for freedom, democracy and anti-war sentiment. Author and historian Chris McNab tells us that the 'remembrance poppy does not attempt to glorify or romanticise conflict but instead, at least once a year, obliges everyone to think about the consequences of war, past, present and future'.[3] In the blurb for his *The Book of the Poppy*, published on the centenary, with the support of the British Legion, McNab writes: 'the poppy compels us to remember war's dead, wounded and bereaved, regardless of nationality or conflict'. This sentiment is echoed in many of the books published during the centenary period. But from the outset the poppy was always political. It was not an anti-war symbol and was never meant to commemorate all the dead of the war. It was never meant to be an international or anti-war symbol. It was meant to rally more people to war, a partisan emblem, designed to commemorate only one side – the victorious British, Americans and their allies. In order to get at the truth, we need to go back to where it all started. Lieutenant Colonel John McCrae, the Canadian medical officer serving in Ypres, is the starting point. He was also an amateur poet and wrote the poem *In Flanders Fields*. By exploring its origins and development, starting out with this poem, it is easy to show that the poppy has always been, and continues to be, a political symbol that legitimises British militarism.

John McCrae first wrote about the poppy blossoming across Flanders in May 1915, soon after burying a friend who had been killed in action. Inspired by the funeral he had just attended, McCrae started the poem by juxtaposing the death of a man with the birth of the poppies. A while later, the poem appeared in *Punch* magazine and before long was widely read and admired in Britain and allied countries.[4] Like many poets before him, James Fox reminds us that McCrae was 'invoking pastoral imagery as an antithesis to war'. Perhaps that is why the overwhelming majority of the thousands of books and articles written about the poem *In Flanders Fields* associate it with anti-war sentiment and the desire for peace. Anyone who reads beyond the first stanza would see it was not a pacifist poem at all – it is very much a pro-war poem. It is worth repeating the poem in full:

In Flanders Fields the poppies blow
Between the crosses, row on row,
That mark our place; and in the sky
The larks, still bravely singing, fly
Scarce heard amidst the guns below.

We are the Dead. Short days ago
We lived, felt dawn, saw sunset glow
Loved and were loved, and now we lie
In Flanders Fields.

Take up your quarrel with the foe:
To you from failing hands we throw
The torch; be yours to hold up high.
If ye break faith with us who die
We shall not sleep, though poppies grow
In Flanders Fields.

John McCrae's *In Flanders Fields* is responsible for establishing the cultural connection between poppies and the Great War.[5] This is not a pacific association, but a call to the living to avenge the deaths of allied soldiers. This poem does not condemn war but legitimises it. It does not demand an end to the war but rather a continuance of war. It is perhaps a testament to the success of pro-war, pro-militarism propaganda and the decline of anti-war, anti-militarism politics in Britain today that *In Flanders Fields* can sound as if it is a pacifist anthem. This author and solider was more than happy to see his poem used as a propaganda tool to aid recruitment drives that would see more young men sign up and die in the trenches.[6]

Despite the over emotional treatment of *In Flanders Fields*, in most history books, everything John McCrae did had the hallmarks of imperialism. His participation in the Boer War, his sense of history, his nationalism, his militarism, his friendship with staunch imperialists and his behaviour during the war were all indicators of a pro-war mentality and opposition to even the mildest of pacifism. [7]

When during the war Pope Benedict brought forward peace proposals, McCrae criticised him. When the Archbishop of Quebec talked peace, McCrae ridiculed him. He talked of his hatred for, and inability to touch or shake the hand of, any German. As young men lay dying in the trenches, he openly expressed satisfaction that his poem was being used extensively in propaganda to further the war effort – for recruiting more men to the trenches, raising money and attacking pacifists. When, in late 1916, President Wilson of the United States tried to persuade the parties in favour of the war to state at the very least why they were fighting, McCrae was virulent in his condemnation, calling him an ass. Rather than end the bloodbath of war, McCrae wanted more dead Germans.[8]

The seminal poem which is inextricably linked to remembrance season and the poppy was being used by the supporters of war: 'Take up your quarrel with the foe.' This was the sentiment being pushed. Full steam ahead with the war was the cry as McCrae's uncompromising words were used to rally ever more men to the killing fields, to butcher and maim the foe or themselves be slaughtered in their youth. Recruiting posters and billboards went up everywhere in Britain, Canada and elsewhere with a picture of the battlefields, a headline 'Our Glorious Deed' and underneath, the words:

If ye break faith with us who die
We shall not sleep, though poppies grow
In Flanders Fields.

The message was clear. John McCrae's poem was being used to

guilt trip young men who may have had doubts or reservations about war. Shame on you if you don't pick up a rifle was the message being conveyed. It has to be asked: just how many young men did John McCrae's poem and the propagandistic use of it send to their death?

When opposition to the war grew, especially in Quebec, over proposed conscription, McCrae expressed anger at his fellow countrymen for giving ground. When Lord Lansdowne, the ex-foreign secretary, published his own, now famous, letter suggesting meaningful victory may no longer have been possible for either side, questioning if the war should continue, McCrae was scathing. He dismissed any suggestion that perhaps it was time to end the bloodshed.[9]

John F. Prescott, in his biography of John McCrae, records that:

> Before he died, McCrae knew his poem to be the most popular of the English-language war verses…He was pleased by its effects in the Empire and the United States…It was the poem of the British army. It was quoted everywhere – with frenzy in selling war bonds and encouraging recruiting with conviction and in harassing pacifists.[10]

The story we are told these days is that 100 years ago terrible, unspeakable things happened, but we were in it together and a centenary marking the end of that war is a good time to commemorate together. But at the heart of official remembrance in Britain is a bad faith. Britain did not fight the good fight for freedom. We were not all in it together. The red poppy emblem was not remembering both sides killed in war. It was never intended as any type of pacifist symbol but rather was a partisan emblem from its inception.

No doubt John McCrae was a brave, principled person, a man of strong Presbyterian faith and sense of duty. But there is no getting away from the fact that principles and politics he advocated were responsible for the loss of countless lives. He supported imperialism and was an unapologetic advocate of wars to defend British imperial interests. He stood full square in the tradition of ardent colonialists like Kipling, Strathcona, Milner and Grey. Those who choose to wear a red poppy can do so, but it is myopic to ignore the fact that the poppy originated in and is stained with the blood of millions of men. They may not have marched off and died in that unnecessary war but for the drum beating of arch imperialists like McCrae and his fellow travellers. There are many politicians, writers and historians who line up to praise the man whose poem is inextricably linked to the origins of poppy imagery and remembrance. They argue, like ex-Prime Minister David Cameron and Conservative Michael Gove, that such men believed they were fighting for democracy against evil. At least McCrae was honest about his imperialism even if the consequence was Passchendaele, Arras, Hill 70, Verdun, Vimy Ridge, the Somme and other mass killing grounds of the First World War. Yet the tragedy is that supporters of British imperialism opposed any attempts to end this slaughter unless on the absolute terms of the British Empire. In the last paragraph on the last page of his excellent biography of John McCrae, John F Prescott concludes by saying:

> This book is a further reminder that militarism and war are never answers to the dilemmas of the human condition.[11]

Sadly, imperialists like McCrae thought they were the answer. That is why it is so important to trace the dubious origins of the poppy and the way we are being asked to remember conflicts via official remembrance today. Though there were many principled anti-war activists who took great risks to oppose the slaughter of the First World War, sadly it was not enough. Failure to successfully challenge this carnage allowed not only for a drawn-out war, but also for British imperialism to pursue reactionary wars for most of the next 100 years largely unchallenged at home. If one cares about such needless loss of life, then the logical conclusion must be an unambiguous critique of the red poppy and its origins. For example, when in recent years the British Legion have used *In Flanders Fields* as part of their poppy campaign, it should be challenged for the warmongering message that it is. When school kids are asked to recite it by heart, we should take the opportunity to engage with young people, to point out the poppy's pro-war origins in order that they make a fully informed judgement.

The Bank of Canada introduced a newly designed $10 bill based on the theme 'Remembrance and Peacekeeping', which included the first verse of John McCrae's poem. It prompted scores of complaints and debate from the people who maintained that the poem had been misprinted, that the first line should read: 'In Flanders Fields the poppies grow'.

The truth being that the Bank of Canada got it right: the first line should indeed read: 'In Flanders Fields the poppies blow'.

It seems ironic that the dispute centred around the words 'grow' or 'blow', rather than the real problem with the poem on the bill – the false association of the First World War poem and the poppy with peace. For anti-war campaigners it is just such examples of the rewriting of history that must be challenged in order to make clear the real origins of the poppy.

It was Moina Michael who made McCrae's poem the centre of the Remembrance Day commemorations. She had read *In Flanders Fields* as the allies were finalising their victory in November 1918 and was convinced that the war's outcome had vindicated the author's rallying cry. She felt compelled to respond to McCrae's final imploring stanza:

Take up your quarrel with the foe:
To you from failing hands we throw

The torch; be yours to hold up high.
If ye break faith with us who die
We shall not sleep, though poppies grow

In the poem she penned in response, *We Shall Keep the Faith*, her clear intention was to retrospectively affirm and defend McCrae's war cry while at the same time saluting the fallen. Deploying the imagery of the blood red poppy, her words were intended to sway the people away from the conclusion that the war had been an entirely senseless waste of life. As historian Nicholas Saunders puts it, 'she hoped [it] would ease the conscience of so many who were wondering why the war had been fought, why so many young men had died'.[12]

The poem was not intended to remember everyone who died in the war. It was in effect a victory poem. The poem makes clear that the victors had 'caught the torch' that had been thrown and 'kept the faith' when others had doubts. This poem was designed to shore up doubters who thought the war was unjustified. It was a retrospective justification of the plea to fight on until Germany was crushed. As James Fox put it, 'Michael, in short, was implying that the war's many casualties were justified because they had been in the service of victory.'[13]

That is why Michael records in her book *The Miracle Flower* that her poem *We Shall Keep The Faith* was referred to by many of her contemporaries as 'The Victory Emblem'.

History records that a short time after responding to John McCrae's poem, Moina Michael's initiative to make the poppy a memorial flower had succeeded across France by 1920 and Canada, Australia, New Zealand and Britain by 1921. No red poppies are sold in Germany, and the anniversary of the end of the war goes unmarked there – 11 November is the feast of St Martin as it is in most of Europe.

As Fox wryly notes, all of the countries that adopted the poppy were victors:

The poppy never found its way into the cultural practices of the war's defeated nations, and that may be because the only men whose sacrifice was believed to deserve such a symbol were those who had fought on the 'right' side. Poppies, in other words, had been converted into victory medals.[14]

If there are any lingering doubts about the partisan origins of the memorial poppy, then one need only name the person responsible for its official promotion in Britain: Field Marshall Douglas Haig. The man whose military decisions led to Flanders poppies being stained with blood and who had a vested interest in justifying the conflict, now had control of the narrative of remembrance, by way of the poppy. The poppy was conceived as a justification of the war and used to celebrate allied victory. It was a political and bellicose symbol from the start. It began with McCrae, continued with Michael and reached new heights of imperialist chauvinism under the stewardship of Douglas Haig and the British ruling elite. Ever since, official remembrance has looked two ways. It mourns the dead and regrets their loss. At the same time, it glorifies their 'necessary sacrifice'. 'The war was terrible', the argument goes, but it was 'a price worth paying for freedom', the mantra continues. The problem, however, is that this line of argument relies on historical amnesia or a dishonest rewriting of history. The reality is that the poppy is a political symbol, born out of a desire to promote, prolong and propagandise the not-so-Great War.

Chapter Two

The Great War

There was nothing great about the Great War.

Over 4 years the armies of the Entente – France, Britain, Russia – and the Alliance – Germany, Austria, Turkey – waged war, killing nearly 10 million combat troops. Nearly 7 million civilians died in the fighting or from starvation and disease because of the destruction. Another 5 million died in a mass influenza epidemic just after the war, so that the total lives lost is around 20 million. Around 23 million troops were wounded in the war, many disabled for the rest of their lives. As men were killed in the trenches and detention camps they left their mothers and fathers, widows and orphans, family and friends bereaved. Most of the men in the armies of the Entente and the Alliance did not want to fight. They were dragooned into the ranks, by conscription, under threat of imprisonment or execution; or they were bullied into volunteering. Some chose to sign up, but many of those regretted that choice later on – if they were lucky.

The course of the war

The two main theatres of war were the Western Front and the Eastern Front.

The Western Front was formed with the 'Battle of the Frontiers' – many battles in which Germany overran Belgian, and then French towns in August 1914, including battles at Lorraine, the Ardennes, Charleroi and Mons – in the Battle of the Frontiers casualties were 329,000 French, 25,597 British, 4500 Belgians. German casualties were 215,594.

The **Battle of the Marne** was the turning point of the Battle of the Frontiers: an army of just over 1 million mostly French troops stopped the advancing German army of nearly 1.5 million. France's casualties (wounded and dead) were 85,000 and German casualties 67,700. Britain had a smaller force in the battle and suffered 1701 casualties.

The **Battle of Ypres** ran from 19 October to 22 November. German and Entente forces fought over the Belgian city at the cost of 145,000 Entente casualties and 47,000 German casualties (though other operations in Belgian cost many more German casualties).

The **Battle of Verdun** went on from 21 February to 18 December 1916. In the hills over the French city of Verdun, Germany and France fought an inconclusive battle for control that lasted nearly a year – 'a lengthy period of general insanity', Field Marshall Lord Allenby called it. Germany's army was 1.25 million, of whom 350,000 became casualties (143,000 of whom were killed). France's army was 100,000 fewer, and their casualties were 400,000 (of whom 159,000 were killed).

The **Somme offensive** was launched on 1 July and ran till 18 November 1916. A joint British-French force (with the support of Canada, Australia, New Zealand and South Africa) attacked German positions on the River Somme. Planned before the German attack at Verdun it was supposed to be a general assault that would push the Central Powers back – but on the eve of the battle Chief Intelligence Officer Brigadier John Charteris admitted, 'we do not expect any great advance', and, 'we are fighting primarily to wear down the German armies and nation'.[1]

At the end of the day on 1 July, in the Battle of the Somme, British forces suffered 60,000 casualties – 20,000 were killed outright. The 36th (Ulster) Division had suffered over 4900 casualties: 86 officers and 1983 other ranks killed or missing; 102 officers and 2626 other ranks wounded. On the same day the Accrington Pals, 700 strong, were sent into combat for the first time: 238 were killed immediately and 350 wounded. 'The powers that be are getting a little uneasy with regard to the situation,' wrote Sir William Robertson, Chief of the Imperial General Staff, as the battle ground on: 'the casualties are mounting up and ministers are wondering whether we are likely to get a proper return for them'.[2] The Somme was the largest battle of the war and cost more than 1 million wounded or dead: 420,000 British casualties, 200,000 French casualties and around 470,000 German casualties.

Nivelle Offensive, 16 April-9 May 1917, was based on an ambitious plan to 'break through' the German line. French casualties were 118,000-187,000, and British 160,000; Germany suffered 163,000 casualties. The high cost of the attack led to mutinies in the French Army, and Nivelle's replacement by Petain.

Messines Ridge, 7-14 June 1917: A British Empire force of 216,000 attacked a force of 126,000 in German positions at Messines-

Looking over the 45-metre crater left by the Messines explosion

Wytschaete Ridge, which they re-took after setting off 21 tons of explosives dug under the enemy trenches. The explosion was so great that it was heard in Dublin. The Empire forces suffered casualties of 24,562 and the Germans 25,000 – 10,000 in the explosion.

Passchendaele, July to November 1917: The battle was fought for control of the ridges south and east of the Belgian city of Ypres between a British Empire force, with support from some French and Belgian Divisions, and a large German army. Estimates of casualties are contested, varying from 200,000-450,000 Entente troops and 200,000-400,000 German troops. British Prime Minister David Lloyd George called it 'one of the greatest disasters of the war' and said that 'no soldier of any intelligence now defends this senseless campaign'. Commander Hubert Gough was blamed for going ahead before the American Expeditionary Force had arrived.

To understand what these millions of lives lost were worth, look at a map and see where the towns of Ypres, Messines and Passchendaele are. Today it would take you half an hour to drive through all three. Another 3 hours would take you down to Verdun in northern France. The Western Front barely moved more than a mile either way for the greater part of the war.

Meanwhile, on the Eastern Front

Where the Western Front was, by the winter of 1914, fixed, the Eastern Front was endlessly churned up. The Austrian Army was not well led, but German forces cut through Russia's plans and territory. Total losses for the spring and summer of 1915 amounted to 1,400,000 killed or wounded, while 976,000 had been taken prisoner. On 5 August, with the Russian Army in retreat, Warsaw fell. According to one engineer:

It is hopeless to fight with the Germans, for we are in no

condition to do anything; even the new methods of fighting become the causes of our failure.

General Ruszky agreed:

The present-day demands of military technique are beyond us. At any rate we can't keep up with the Germans. (August 1914)

In July 1915 the ministers chanted:

Poor Russia! Even her army, which in past ages filled the world with the thunder of its victories...Even her army turns out to consist only of cowards and deserters.[3]

In answer to alarmed questions from his colleagues as to the situation at the front, the War Minister, Polivanov, answered in these words: 'I place my trust in the impenetrable spaces, impassable mud, and the mercy of Saint Nicholas Mirlikisky, Protector of Holy Russia.' (Session of 4 August 1915).

The Russian Army lost in the whole war more men than any army which ever participated in a national war – approximately 2.5 million killed, or 40 per cent of all the losses of the Entente. According to Aleksandr Pireiko:

Everyone, to the last man, was interested in nothing but peace...Who should win and what kind of peace it would be, that was of small interest to the army. It wanted peace at any cost, for it was weary of war.

Minister of the Interior Nikolay Maklakov feared that the soldiers on leave in Moscow were trouble:

That's a wild crowd of libertines knowing no discipline,

rough-housing, getting into fights with the police (not long ago a policeman was killed by the soldiers), rescuing arrested men, etc. Undoubtedly, in case of disorders this entire horde will take the side of the mob.

Russia's defeats and its own inner turmoil meant that by 1917 it was struggling to keep up the fight, and in October of that year it withdrew altogether.

The final battles on the Western Front

The **Spring Offensive,** 21 March to August 1918: Following the Russian treaty at Brest-Litovsk settling the war in the east, Germany put all its major forces into the Western Front, in an effort to break the deadlock. The push was also known as the Spring Offensive and the 'Kaiser's War', or 'Kaiserschlacht'. German advances into Entente positions were extensive but made at great cost.

There were 688,341 German casualties, 418,374 British and 433,000 French losses. By its end the German predominance on the Western Front was at an end, through its own losses and by the arrival of the American Expeditionary Force. In Germany the Kaiser's War was seen as a last throw of the dice.

The Hundred Days Offensive, 8 August to 11 November 1918. With the arrival of US troops in the summer of 1918 the balance of power shifted to the Entente, the battles that followed saw Germany pushed back out of Belgium and France. The Battle of the Argonne Forest was a major part of the final Allied offensive of the First World War that stretched along the entire Western Front. It was fought from 26 September 1918 until the Armistice of 11 November 1918, a total of 47 days. The Meuse-Argonne Offensive was the largest in US military history, involving 1.2 million American soldiers. The battle cost 28,000 German lives, 26,277 American lives and an unknown number of French lives.

That autumn, the German Army was defeated – but not by the troops of the Entente or the United States of America.

A World War

The Western Front and the Eastern Front were not the only theatres of War. Britain backed Hussein bin Ali, Sharif of Mecca, in his revolt against Ottoman rule, with the forces of the British-Indian Army. The war cost the lives of tens of thousands of Turkish troops, and also plunged Syria, the Lebanon and Palestine into famine.

> People were found in the streets, unconscious, and were carried to hospitals. We passed women and children lying by the roadside with closed eyes and ghastly, pale faces. It was a common thing to find people searching the garbage heaps for orange peel, old bones, or other refuse and eating them greedily when found. Everywhere women could be seen seeking eatable weeds among the grass along the roads.

It was estimated that between 60,000 and 80,000 had died of starvation in northern Syria.[4]

In Africa Paul von Lettow-Vorbeck led a force of European and native troops from German East Africa in a prolonged guerrilla war against British and Portuguese colonial forces. The greatest loss of life was among the native bearers – the 'carrier corps' that both Lettow-Vorbeck and the British were dependent upon.

They waged war against their own men

The conditions of war were onerous and brutalising. On the Western Front men fought from trenches that were often flooded. The bodies of their comrades were often rotting nearby, lost in 'no-man's land'. They were plagued by rats, flies and lice.

All around me the most gruesome devastation. Dead and wounded soldiers, dead and dying animals, horse cadavers, burnt out houses, shell-cratered fields, devastated vehicles, weapons, fragments of uniforms – all this is scattered around me, in total confusion.

Most of all the filth ground men down.

My sacks dangled in the water, the contents became sodden and a tremendous weight. My overcoat (thick) did the same. My upper half became plastered with mud, with constantly slipping against the side of the narrow trench. My rifle, wrapped in sandbags became the same...
German infantryman Paul Hub[5]

Men in the army were brutalised and dominated by violent and autocratic commanding officers. The military is not a democracy. It runs on orders. Basic training was all about breaking men's spirits and getting them to obey orders without question.

They began to flog soldiers for the most trivial offences; for example, for a few hours' absence without leave. And sometimes they flogged them in order to rouse their fighting spirit.
Aleksandr Pireiko

The first clue about the bond between the men and the officers was that the men in the trenches were armed with rifles, the officers with small arms. The officers had pistols to shoot men who would not advance.

The second clue about the bond between the men and the officers was the great many desertions, and later mutinies that wracked the armies of the Entente and the Alliance. Around 100,000 British and German troops called an unofficial ceasefire

The Grumble, Leon Henri Ruffé's engraving of French troops after the Nivelle offensive

on Christmas Eve 1914, to the anger of their commanding officers (and again on Christmas Eve 1915). In Singapore, in 1915, the Muslim Rajput soldiers of the 5th Light Infantry, angered by constant discrimination, mutinied, killing their officers and taking control of the territory. The Russian Army was beset by desertions as troops abandoned the line in their thousands, and in February of 1917 their protests triggered a revolution in Russia – its key demand was an end to the brutalisation of troops by their commanding officers, and also for an end to the war.

In April 1917, after the failure of the 'Nivelle Offensive', and having heard of the Russian mutinies, thousands of French troops mutinied refusing orders to fight – they elected leaders and called for an end to the war. Twenty-seven thousand deserted. Around a thousand men mutinied in the British training ground at Etaples, the 'Bull Ring', in September 1917. In October 1917 the Russian Army again mutinied and again this was part of a larger revolution that took the country out of the war altogether. In the autumn of 1918 the German Navy at Kiel began a mutiny that turned into a revolution, effectively bringing the whole war to an end. Troops deserted and mutinied because they had been pushed to the point of endurance and beyond, and often they turned their bayonets on their commanding officers.

Execution of the Fifth Light Infantry at Singapore

The third clue as to the bond between the officers and the troops is that thousands of men were shot at the orders of their officers for not fighting, either for 'cowardice in the face of the enemy', desertion or mutiny. British court martials had 306 soldiers shot at dawn, of whom 266 were convicted of desertion and 18 of cowardice. Among them were 25 Canadians, 22 Irishmen, 5 New Zealanders and 21 of the Chinese labour corps. French officers executed 600 men for desertion, cowardice in the face of the enemy and other offences. Of the mutineers of the British-Indian Army in Singapore in 1915, 47 were killed by firing squad and a further 64 exiled for life. The German Army records just 18 executed.

'Total War'

Germany's military leader Erich von Ludendorff called the Great War a Total War. He meant that not just the soldiers, but everyone had to do their part, that all society would give to the war effort. That was true. Before the soldiers could be sent over the top into no-man's land all the nations' collective efforts had been mobilised in civilian life as they were in military life.

The war cost lives, and it cost money.

	Dead
British Empire	947,000
French Empire	1,400,000
Germany	1,800,000
Austria-Hungary	1,200,000
Russia	1,700,000
USA	116,000
Italy	65,000

Not only were lives lost to those countries, but the billions spent on the war were wasted too. The cost of the entire war was estimated at £80 billion (five and a half trillion in 2018 sterling) – or enough to give 'every family in America, Canada, Australia, Great Britain and Ireland, France, Belgium, Germany and Russia', estimated Dr Nicholas Butler of the Carnegie Foundation, 'a five-hundred pound house, two hundred pounds worth of furniture, and a hundred pounds worth of land'.[6] A lot of government spending was borrowed money, debts which after the war would sap the European recovery and cause more conflict over who would pay the bills. All that government spending, even if it was on credit, still had a terrible impact on society before the debts were repaid. Every penny spent on munitions and guns commanded resources that otherwise would have been going towards really useful things, like cutlery, bicycles and bread. War spending soaked up all of society's good endeavours and put them instead to waste and destruction. Factories making engines and tools were turned to making bombs and barbed wire. People who were farming the land were sent off to fight. A massive shift took place from producing things that would help people, like food and other consumer goods, and also tools and machines, to working at making things that would kill people.

The amount of food and other necessaries of life was cut right back. Though war industries put more people to work, meaning that more people had a wage packet at the end of the week, the shift from making goods to making weapons meant that all those wage packets were chasing fewer and fewer consumer goods. That mean that inflation shot up, making basics so expensive that people could not afford them; the extra cash in their pockets was worth less. From July 1914 to July 1916, wrote labour economist Maurice Dobb, the official cost of living index rose 45 per cent, where wage rates had only risen some 15 to 20 per cent. In Glasgow, where workers flooded into new munitions factories, no new dwellings were built, so that rents went up.

In Germany ration cards were introduced in February 1915: first bread was rationed (1.5 kg) followed by potatoes (2.5 kg), 80 grams of butter, 250 grams of sugar and half an egg a week: about a third of the calories a person needs. The next winter all food was in short supply, so that it became known as the 'Turnip

British rations explained

Winter'. In Russia baking white bread was forbidden as provision trains failed to reach Moscow and other cities. Rationing came later in Britain, with 2lb of meat, ½ lb of sugar and ½ lb of total fats allowed each a week.[7]

Either through inflation or rationing, consumption was held down, while more people were working in the munitions factories. Propaganda campaigns urged women to help the war effort by reusing their scraps. Local authorities, like Croydon, organised workers' kitchens to save money on food. 'Real wages in Britain fell sharply,' explains historian Adrian Gregory, 'whilst production actually rose.'[8]

One and a half million Indians were recruited into the British-Indian Army, no longer available for farming, and the country was taxed with feeding that army as well as occupied Mesopotamia. In 1918 the strain was too much, prices sky-rocketed and people were starving. Viscount Chelmsford wrote to the Secretary of State for India that, 'stocks of all food grain will barely suffice to meet internal demand'. In some Turkish villages only 15 per cent of those of military age returned and if it were not for the hundreds of thousands of deserters, farm output would have collapsed altogether.[9]

Industrial conscription

There was industrial conscription as well as military conscription. 'We can hardly win a war without the industrial workers,' Undersecretary of State Wahnschaffe wrote to Ludendorff. In February 1915 the 'Committee on Production' was set up in Britain under the Chairmanship of Sir George Askwith, with the aim of finding out how 'after consultation with the representatives of employers and employed as to the best steps to be taken to ensure that the productive power of the employees in engineering and shipbuilding establishments...shall be made fully available to meet the needs of the nation in the present emergency'.[10]

British unions and the government signed a deal at the Treasury outlawing strikes; so did the German unions, on 2 August 1914. Under Britain's War Munitions Act of 1915 munition workers were forbidden from leaving work without the permission of the Ministry of Munitions (or the Admiralty, which managed many of the factories and workshops). Under the 1915 act it was illegal in a 'Controlled Establishment' for anyone to 'restrict output'. The Ministry of Munitions issued employers with 'certificates of exemption' meaning that workers in vital industries could not be conscripted into the army, which meant that they could not leave their work, either.

The Commissioner of the Committee of Inquiry into the Causes of Industrial Unrest found that 'the nerves of the men and their families are raked by hard workshop conditions, low and unfair wages in some cases, deficient housing accommodation, war sorrows and bereavements, excessive prices of food'. He added that 'the authorities were ignoring their grievances and troubles and threatening them instead with Military Service'.[11]

In Germany, on 2 December 1916 the German government brought in the Hilfsdiengesetz – or law of mobilisation – which 'tied the worker to his workplace'. Every man between 17 and 60 not already in the armed forces was made to report to the authorities with a certificate of employment or a certificate from a previous employer. In that latter case he would be directed to a place of work. If he refused, or left his work, he could be imprisoned for a year.[12]

The workforce changed in make-up, too. Between 1914 and 1918, hundreds of British factories were re-tooled to make munitions. Over 890,000 women – teenagers, wives, mothers and grandmothers – joined the 2 million already working in factories. Trade union membership climbed from 6.5 million to 8 million. They filled the gaps left by volunteer and later conscripted servicemen.

In Germany, the BASF chemical factory had 900 Russian and

Polish prisoners of war among its 22,000 strong workforce. When the prisoners acted up, they brought in a 'supervising officer' who, in the words of the internal company records, 'introduced a strict regimen'.[13]

Coercion was common in war industries. When miners at West Cumberland Ore went on strike the government issued an order that those who carry out 'any act calculated or likely to restrict the production' of war material 'are guilty of an offence under the Defence of the Realm Regulations, the punishment for which is penal servitude for life'. As labour activist William Paul argued, 'every nation at present is in reality waging two wars – the national war abroad and the class war at home'.[14]

With their rights to leave work taken away, employees were exposed to exploitative and dangerous conditions. One worker in a small arms factory, Cook, died suddenly, and at the inquest it was found he had been working 80 hours a week. The coroner said that he 'died for his country'. 'There were cases of men working 100 hours a week,' according to labour economist Maurice Dobb, 'and 70 to 80 hours were not uncommon,' while 56 to 60 hours a week was the norm.[15]

The feeling that the work had to be done to protect the men in the trenches was a powerful reason to cut corners when it came to safety. In his memoirs Lloyd George highlighted the case of the women working in munitions who often suffered 'toxic jaundice from TNT poisoning': 'The ailment turned their faces a repulsive yellow' – earning them the nickname of canaries. In 1916 there were 181 cases of TNT poisoning, 53 of which were fatal; 189 cases and 44 deaths in 1917; 34 cases and 10 deaths in 1918. In a factory at Hayes women were put to work hammering defective American shells; 'risky work', said Lloyd George, 'for if a trace of the fulminate were ignited by the blow', the shell 'would explode and disembowel them'.[16]

Thirty-five women were killed in an explosion in 42 Shed, at the Barnbow munitions factory in Leeds, at 10pm on Tuesday 5

December 1916. The National Shell Filling Factory in Chilwell, Nottinghamshire was destroyed in an explosion of 8 tons of TNT on 1 July 1918. In all 134 people were killed, of whom only 32 could be positively identified, and a further 250 were injured. A total of 109 were men, 25 women. Factory manager Lord Chetwynd blamed it on sabotage, but more likely it was the poor safety standards that were to blame.

The Brunner Mond munitions factory in Silvertown exploded on 19 January 1917 – though the news of the extent of the losses was suppressed: on the memorial in the Silvertown Works, just the 16 people in the shed that exploded are listed as dead; Hector Bolitho's biography of Alfred Mond published in 1933 says 40 were killed. Today it is acknowledged that 73 people were killed as the blast tore through the surrounding houses, of which around eight hundred were destroyed. Brunner Mond were compensated £185,000 for their loss of earnings by the UK Government.[17]

The African Carrier Corps were forced to work under the British Empire's Native Followers Recruitment Ordinance

Forced labour was more naked in the treatment of colonial and foreign workers. Britain and France recruited Chinese labourers under an agreement with Finance Minister Liang Shiyi to supply

300,000. The men were contracted under indentures that lasted for 5 years. Once they had signed on they were under military discipline as the Chinese Labour Corps (CLC), and imprisoned in barracks, working 10 hours a day, 7 days a week. The work was dangerous – 752 were killed when their ship, the Athos, was hit by a German torpedo, and news of their deaths was suppressed at the time. Researcher Chen Ta for the US Bureau of Labor Statistics listed 25 riots and strikes by CLC workers between November 1916 and July 1917. Of the 140,000 labourers sent to France, 10,000 died. Twenty-one of them were executed for mutiny.[18]

In Africa 'the British had in 1915 passed the Native Followers Recruitment Ordinance, a law that allowed for compulsory recruitment of men from across British ruled Africa to work as carriers'. By the end of 1917 more men in the British colonies that bordered German East Africa had served as carriers than had not. Around 250,000 men died servicing the British war effort in Africa, and another 120,000 died as carriers to Paul von Lettow-Vorbeck's East Africa force. They died from exhaustion, infected wounds and other diseases, weakened by malnutrition. They were slaves.[19]

'Prussianism'

Democracy, which was in any case limited, was largely suspended throughout the war. Governments of national unity avoided elections or any open debate about war aims. Laws were passed to silence opponents of the war, like the Defence of the Realm Act (DORA) in Britain and the Military Service (No. 2) Act. Under DORA the offices of both the moderate peace campaign, the Union for Democratic Control, and the more radical No-Conscription Fellowship were raided in 1916. The laws demanded that all leaflets and papers carried the names of the publisher and author, so that they could be prosecuted.

In 1904 the British Army had set up a press bureau to monitor the newspapers, and in January 1916 'the press bureau had been re-established as bureau M17a (censorship) responsible to the Director of Military Intelligence, General McDonogh'. M17b, meanwhile, was hived off to work with the Foreign Office, producing foreign propaganda.[20]

Anti-conscription posters, the Guildford chief constable was advised, were to be torn down or defaced. Those posting them, his South Shield counterpart was instructed, should be advised that their actions would appear to contravene DRR 27, a catch-all regulation dealing with the expression of views prejudicial to the conduct of the war, and should be stopped. If necessary, legal actions were to be taken against such persons.[21]

Suffragette Sylvia Pankhurst, Glasgow socialists John McLean, Willie Gallacher and John William Muir, liberal philosopher Bertrand Russell were all detained under DORA. Many more less well-known activists faced prison, too, as Brock Millman explained: 'Oxford undergraduate Alan Kaye was sentenced to 2 months' imprisonment in 1916 for distributing "Shall Britons Be Conscripts?"' 'Clara Cole and Rosa Hobhouse', who had organised a peace pilgrimage, 'were arrested and sentenced to 5 months' imprisonment'. R. V. Cox, another No-Conscription Fellowship member, was tried for selling their paper *The Tribunal.* No publisher would touch *The Tribunal* after the press bureau threatened them, so it was run off on a roneo machine.[22] The No-Conscription Fellowship's Fenner Brockway was arrested four times and spent most of the latter war years in Walton prison, while chairman Clifford Allen was arrested three times, his health collapsing in 1917. Meetings organised by the No-Conscription Fellowship were regularly banned, or the venue owners rung by the police and persuaded to cancel the meeting.

In Germany in the autumn of 1914, authorities banned

meetings of anti-war socialists in Stuttgart, Munchen-Gladbag, Liepzig and Altona. Radical newspapers like the *Rheinische Zeitung,* the *Volksblatt* and the *Echo vom Rheinfall* were ordered to close. The Social Democratic paper *Vorwarts* was closed in September and only allowed to reopen the following month when the editors promised not to mention the 'class struggle'.[23] Leading socialists were imprisoned, including Rosa Luxemburg, Karl Liebknecht, Ernest Meyer and Franz Mehring. Despite being an elected deputy in the Reichstag, Liebknecht was sentenced to four-and-a-half years in prison.

Before the war, Britain, Germany and France were democracies – with some pointed restrictions. But for the duration, they became dictatorships that silenced dissent with jail time, suspended Parliamentary debate, censored the Press and seized suspect literature.

Fighting back

Two years before the Great War started, the socialist parties of Europe met in Basel. There they agreed to oppose war between their states – a policy they had first set out in 1907 – and even to call a general strike to prevent the war. But on 4 August 1914 both the German and the French socialists in their respective parliaments voted in favour of war budgets. The Socialist International was shattered by the war, as the brotherhood of man gave way to German, French, British and Austrian socialists turning their guns against each other.

Many socialists, like Keir Hardie, Ramsay MacDonald and Jean Jaures were opposed to the war. Some, like Karl Liebknecht, Rosa Luxemburg, James Connolly, John McLean and V. I. Lenin were set to make a revolution against it. But the majority of the socialist leaders, men like Arthur Henderson in Britain (whose sons were in the army), railwaymen's leader Jimmy Thomas and even the firebrand Victor Grayson backed the war; so did Belgian socialist Emile Vandervelde and Sweden's Hjalmar Branting, and

Pierre Renaudel of France. Years of lobbying their own domestic governments for reforms led these men to embrace patriotism.

In the summer and autumn of 1914 those few hold outs who were against the war were isolated, and on the defensive. But such was the strain that war placed on the whole of society, that in time the anti-war activists were speaking to large crowds of angry men and women. Over the next 3 years there were more and more protests and strikes over different features of life under war time. The war put tremendous stress on society, curbing wages, demanding more labour, threatening famine and wasting lives. All that stress provoked protests and revolts. Many of these conflicts were not in the first place protests against the war. But even where they were not, governments tended to cast them as if they were. Strikers were told that they were siding with the enemy. Protestors were put under martial law. Reacting against war time conditions, more and more people began to protest against the war itself – at which point governments lost control.

In 1915, 200,000 Welsh miners went out on strike against the Munitions Act, which they thought was dictatorship. The strike was remarkable in that it was wholly political, against the war measure, not provoked by any change in their day-to-day terms and conditions. That year Mary Barbour and Andrew MacBride organised a great rent strike in Glasgow. The rent strike led to the formation of the Clyde Workers Committee, which gathered shop stewards in the engineering plants and docks. The Clyde Workers Committee launched a number of strikes over pay and working conditions. When Munitions Minister David Lloyd George went to Glasgow to talk to the strikers, he was booed in a great public hall (nine days later, Scottish socialists John Maclean and James Maxton were jailed in revenge).

Assistant Secretary to the Cabinet William Ormsby-Gore fulminated that 'the essence of this movement is, of course, the new form of Marxian syndicalism, revolutionary in its aims and methods, aiming at the overthrow of the existing social and economic order by direct action'. Ormsby-Gore warned that:

> the leaders, whether Jew or Irish, have this common feature, they are all men with dissatisfied national aspirations, embittered against society and bent on using the results of the war to overthrow the existing order of things.[24]

The *Times* editorialised: 'We must deal as harshly with strikers who throw down their tools as with soldiers who desert in the field.'[25]

On 28 May 1915 more than a thousand women demonstrated for peace in front of the Reichstag. That November women demonstrated in Stuttgart against the high cost of living, while police in Liepzig were called out to put down food riots. In Berlin there were protests and fighting outside of empty shops in February 1916. Then in May the small Internationale group of socialists called a demonstration against the 'imperialist war'. Karl Liebknecht published a popular leaflet with the headline, 'the main enemy is at home' – meaning that it was the bosses that were the true enemies of the German workers, not the French and British soldiers in the trenches. Thousands rallied around Liebknecht at the Potsdamer Platz. When he was arrested, 55,000 Berlin munitions workers, led by Richard Müller, came out on strike.[26]

On the front line, German soldiers wrote back home, but their letters were intercepted by the censors: they called for peace, said that the war was a capitalist war, and that 'at home they must strike and strike hard, and cause a revolution, and then peace must come'.[27]

The most audacious blow against the war recruitment drive was struck in Ireland in Easter 1916. There the moderate Irish nationalist leader John Redmond had pledged the Irish Volunteers to the British war drive in the hope of winning Home Rule when peace came. Soon it became clear that the Irish recruits in the British Army would still be second-class citizens to their British officers (many of whom were Ulster loyalists with a special hatred for Irish Catholics). After the losses in Gallipoli and with a steady depletion of Irish men, the feeling that they were cannon fodder in a British imperial war became stronger. A group within the volunteers opposed the war and organised themselves independently. Their leaders – Patrick Pearse, Tom Clarke, Seán MacDermott, Joseph Plunkett, Éamonn Ceannt and Thomas MacDonagh, along with James Connolly's Irish Citizens Army – launched a pre-emptive rebellion in Ireland seizing the Post Office in Dublin to announce a republic. For a week the Irish rebels fought to hold Dublin, while the might of the British Empire turned away from the Western Front to try to take back what had been a part of the United Kingdom just a month earlier. The suppression of the rebellion cost thousands of lives, and demolished central Dublin. But the execution of the leaders of the Rising only strengthened hostility to Britain, so that much of the country was in open opposition to the war, to conscription and to the continuation of British rule. The Socialist International's hope for a general strike against the war in Europe was disappointed in 1914, but in April of 1918 Irish workers, with the support of Sinn Fein, did organise such a strike. That, along with the Anti-Conscription Protests, stopped the application of conscription in Ireland throughout the war, while it went ahead on the British mainland.

In February 1917 a women's day protest in St Petersburg quickly escalated into an all-out general strike across the city. Textile and munitions workers joined to paralyse the city. They protested against the Tsar, against the war and against its hardships. Soldiers back from the front joined the protests. A panicked Tsar ordered the fearsome Cossack troops to clear the protests, but even those hardened reactionaries would not charge the women in the streets. The Tsar's power ebbed but he resisted calls to abdicate until it was clear that he was no longer in charge anyway. No ruling power existed apart from the workers' councils – 'soviets' – that the protestors gathered in. Without much confidence the liberal politicians who had cowered under the Tsar before called themselves a Provisional Democratic Government, under the leadership of the moderate socialist Kerensky. To win the confidence of the French and British ambassadors, Kerensky promised to keep up Russia's part in the war, but it was a promise that would prove fatal to his government.

Over the summer the provisional government struggled to keep the initiative. Though they called themselves democrats, they avoided calling elections, for fear that they would be thrown out. By the autumn local election results gave majorities instead to the anti-war 'Bolsheviks'. The 'soviets' that the workers and soldiers set up to represent their interests did not give way to the new provisional government but carried on, creating a 'dual power' between the masses' and the middle classes' rival governing institutions.

Kerensky called on the military to suppress the Bolsheviks, only to panic when it became clear that General Kornilov planned to overthrow him, too. To stop Kornilov the soviets created a Military Revolutionary Committee tasked with defending the February Revolution. Kerensky never did call an election to give his provisional government a mandate. When an All-Russian Soviet Congress was planned Kerensky again tried to use the military to stop it. Kerensky's Foreign Minister Pavel Milyukov said:

The bourgeois republic, defended only by socialists of moderate tendencies, finding no longer any support in the masses...could not maintain itself. Its whole essence had evaporated. There remained only an external shell.

The fate of the Kerensky government was necessarily the same as that of the tsarist monarchy: 'Both prepared the ground for a revolution, and on the day of revolution neither could find a single defender.' The Military Revolutionary Committee overthrew Kerensky and supported a Soviet Government, led by the Bolsheviks.[28]

In January 1918 the Austrian government cut flour rations, and the workers at the Daimler factory in Wiener Neustadt walked out. The strike snow-balled, with 200,000 out on 17 January and by 19 January Vienna workers were joined by miners in Ostrau, Brno, Pilsen, Prague and Steiermark. In Budapest, a general strike paralysed the city. The Viennese authorities quickly gave in. The strikers' success inspired Berlin, where 400,000 went on strike on 28 January. They were followed by strikes in Dusseldorf, Kiel, Hamburg and Cologne, with around 4 million out in total. The protests were only stopped when the German government declared a 'state of siege', rounding up the ringleaders to try them in courts martial. One hundred and fifty were imprisoned and nearly 50,000 sent into the army and packed off to the Western Front.[29]

All of these actions can be seen as if they were merely reactions to social conditions, just spontaneous or mechanical reactions. But in truth all of these protests were made by people who, in different ways, decided they had had enough. Those people were not acting in a vacuum. They could see – or read about – what was happening in the rest of the world. The French mutinies after the Nivelle offensive failed were self-consciously modelled on the February Revolution in Russia, even to the point of organising 'soldiers councils' to argue their case. The workers' strikes in Germany were inspired by the Russian October Revolution. The Russian revolutionists were watching the revolts in Budapest and Germany, hoping that these would give them more support. The anti-war leaders in Britain, John Maclean and Sylvia Pankhurst, campaigned for the new Soviet Union against its enemies and were rewarded with positions as ambassadors of the New Society.

How the war really ended

Russia's February Revolution gave Germany's military leaders hope, but it also inspired opponents of the war. The 'German proletariat must draw the lessons of the Russian Revolution and take their own destiny in hand', said Fritz Heckert of the far-left Spartacist group. The Minister of the Interior bemoaned 'the intoxicating effect of the Russian Revolution'.[30]

On the cruiser *Friedrich der Grosse*, a stoker, Willy Sachse, and a sailor, Max Reichpietsch, started a discussion group of socialists. On shore at Wilhelmshaven they talked to other ships crews and other canteen committees were set up making a secret League of Soldiers and Sailors.

Reichpietsch went to the Socialist Party headquarters for help but was told that it was against their policy to recruit in the armed forces. 'We ought to stand in shame before these sailors,' party organiser Luise Zietz said, 'they are much more advanced than we are.'

The 'Flottenzentrale' – a secret committee to coordinate 5000 sailors was set up on 25 July 1917. Their slogan was 'Arise! Let us break our chains as the Russians have done!' In August 1917 the ships the *Prinz Regent Luitpold* and the *Pillau* were in open revolt. Hundreds of men walked off. The authorities rounded up the ringleaders and Reichpietsch and Alwin Köbis were executed on 5 September. Watching these events in Russia, Lenin saw them as 'a great turning point' and 'the eve of a worldwide revolution' – words he put into deeds shortly after with the October Revolution.

The Russian revolutionaries had their own challenges, but they were committed internationalists and set about promoting a revolutionary end to the war. Karl Radek, a socialist leader in Poland and in the German SPD before leaving for Russia, became Vice Commissar for Foreign Affairs in the new government. He organised German socialists from among the prisoners of war held by the Russians, who put out a German language journal *Die Fackel* ('The Torch'). German soldiers and workers should turn on their own generals and bosses to bring the war to an end was its message.

In Germany the different socialist leaders were generally sceptical – Bernstein and Kautsky (who were often the targets of Lenin's polemics) rubbished the Russian Revolution, and even Rosa Luxemburg was unsure. But actions spoke louder than words. The Manfred Weiss armaments factory in Budapest was struck out and strikes broke out across Austria-Hungary. German workers were immediately moved by the Bolshevik Revolution. A massive strike wave broke out across Germany in January 1918. 'Workers' councils' were set up in Vienna and Berlin. A Spartacist leaflet lauded 'the workers councils of Vienna elected on the Russian model' and announced a general strike beginning on 28 January. Five hundred thousand were on strike in Berlin, led by activists like metalworkers' leader Richard Müller. The trams were shut down. The socialist leaders condemned the action. Ebert told the crowd at Treptow Park: 'it is the duty of the workers to support their brothers and their fathers who are at the front and to make the best possible weapons for them'. Just to emphasise the point he added, 'as the English and French workers are doing for their brothers at the front'. The strikers were left high and dry by the socialists they thought would lead them and they drifted back to work. Between March and November 1918 nearly 200,000 Germans were killed in the war.

Despite the collapse of the January strikes, the Bolshevik revolution continued to stand as a model of how to end the war for the mass of Germans. Veteran socialist Franz Mehring spoke out in favour of the Bolsheviks saying they were the true inheritors of the socialist tradition. The SPD leadership could not contain what they called 'the romantic taste for the Bolshevik revolution'. The more radical Spartacist group was making headway in the major cities. The moderate socialists in the Cabinet pressed for the release of Karl Liebknecht, fearing that his imprisonment would become a cause celebre for the growing radical movement. Out of prison he went straight from the Potsdam station to a rally calling for a Russian Revolution in Germany. By October workers were setting up revolutionary councils at the Daimler plant in Stuttgart and the Zeppelin plant in Friedrichschafen. Labour activists Richard Müller and Hugo Haase fixed the date of the Revolution for 11 November.

At Kiel sailors were hearing that they were to ready for a general offensive. On board the ships, they protested, and about a thousand men were arrested and disembarked. On 1 November sailors met at the trade union centre at Kiel, led by Karl Artelt, and called a demonstration for the third. The demonstration was banned, but many went ahead. An armed patrol opened fire and nine people were killed, 29 wounded. That night Artelt set up a 'sailors council' on a torpedo boat which rallied some 20,000 on different ships. The officers were overwhelmed and straight away started giving in to the men's demands – to abolish saluting, for shore leave and so on. Before long Kiel was under the command of the sailors' council. They appealed for help, and at Wilhelmshaven a workers' and soldiers' council, led by the stoker Bernhard Kuhnt, called a general strike. The strikes were supported in Berlin and Hamburg. In a panic the socialist

The November Revolution in Germany

leaders reversed their position and called for the abdication of the Kaiser and an Armistice.

The Great War was started by statesmen and generals, thoughtlessly and hysterically defending their honour with the waste of other people's lives. The war was brought to an end by different people. With sober senses the opponents of the war, in Dublin in Easter 1916, in St Petersburg in February 1917, and again in October 1917 – and in Kiel, Wilhelmshaven and Berlin in November 1918 – organised the mass of the people to stop the war. On 9 November the government announced the Kaiser's abdication. On 11 November a German delegation signed the Armistice before France's General Foch. The war was over.

Chapter Three

Why was there a War?

The Great War was a vast human sacrifice of 20 million human beings, at a cost estimated at 80 billion sterling, and the exhaustion of billions of man hours – often woman hours – of effort in the munitions factories. The end-point was...what? Were the rights of small nations protected? Small nations were overrun, occupied and reoccupied throughout the war. Was authoritarian 'Prussianism' defeated? In the 20 years that followed authoritarian governments dominated Europe. Was it, as they said, the 'war to end all wars'? Just 20 years later all Europe was plunged into another world war, so that the Great War had to be re-named 'World War One'.

Trying to explain the war was not easy for politicians at the time, or for historians since. That is not because it is complicated. It is because the reasons the war was fought were too shameful to the leaders who pitched us into it. Rather than face the truth of their own complicity, understanding the Great War is wreathed in lies, half-truths and wilful misunderstandings. Underneath those lie the true story of why the war was fought.

The assassination of the Archduke Ferdinand

The first and most obvious explanation for the Great War is that it started with the assassination of the Archduke Ferdinand, in Sarajevo. On this account a teenager, Gavrilo Princip, part of a small guerrilla band hoping to free Bosnia, assassinated Franz Ferdinand, heir to the Habsburg Throne, leading Austria to exact humiliating conditions from the Serbian Government (who were not responsible), provoking the Russian Tsar to threaten to mobilise military action against Austria, which in turn led the German government to threaten action against Russia, but to take it against Russia's ally France, pre-emptively, marching through Belgium, whose neutrality Britain was committed to defending, leading them to join Russia and France in declaring war against Germany and Austria; in the melee, the Ottoman War Minister Enver Pasha bombarded Russian positions with the help of German battleships, so that war was declared there also.

This improbable sequence of events explains very little, like pushing on a chain. Princip, who lived to see it from his prison cell, was asked how he felt about starting a world war. If I had not done it, the Germans would have found another excuse, the Balkan freedom fighter replied.[1] Princip was right. His crew were only the proximate cause of the war, not its underlying reason; the spark that ignited a powder keg, in a cellar packed with high explosives.

Each step on the march could have led another way if the statesmen, ambassadors, ministers, generals, kings and Caesars had not reacted in the ways they did. Far from being determined to avenge the wrong that Serbia – or the lad Princip, anyway – had committed, 'it was only rather reluctantly and under German pressure the Austro-Hungarian ministers recommended that the Emperor Franz Joseph finally to sign the order for a general mobilisation on 31 July' 1914, James Joll explains. So, too, was Russian minister Savonov firmed up in his decision to wage war by the urgent treaties of the French ambassador Paleologue. Germany's eventual decision to invade through Belgium was made under the firm belief that Britain would stay neutral, as Britain's Foreign Minister Lord Grey had promised to Prince Lichnowsky, the German ambassador in London.[2]

The war as 'a series of unfortunate events' also downplays the way that the system of treaties locked in a destructive dynamic. At first the Great Powers entered into treaties with one another as a way of trying to control the competitive, anarchic interplay of rival states. These treaties it was hoped would off-set the dangers inherent in an uncontrolled international system. The British ambition was to maintain the balance of power, which really meant to make sure that none of the other states became powerful enough to challenge her. For most of the nineteenth century, Britain was in direct rivalry with France, and allied herself to whichever states were opposed to France – including Germany, whose colonial ambitions in Africa Britain supported. When Germany's economic might and military sway challenged continental domination, Britain instead allied herself with France.

France, too, allied itself with Russia, as a counterweight to German influence, as Germany's alliance with Austria, and with Turkey, was intended to balance the threat from France and from Russia. The alliances that were initially sought to contain the conflicts came to have the opposite effect, amplifying the conflicts. 'Once the governments of Europe came to believe that they were aligned in two rival camps, then the winning of an additional small state to their side seemed to be of great importance,' wrote historian James Joll: 'The existence of the alliance system above all conditioned expectations about the form a war would take if it broke out, and about who were likely to be friends and who enemies.'

Alliances were also secretive, as military alliances they were often not open to public scrutiny. Lloyd George remembered that:

There is no more conspicuous example of this kind of suppression of vital information than the way in which military arrangements were entered into with France and were kept from the Cabinet for six years. There is abundant evidence that both the French and Russians regarded these military arrangements as practically tantamount to a commitment on our part to come to the aid of France in the event of her being attacked by Germany...Yet the Cabinet were never informed of these vital arrangements until we were so deeply involved in the details of the military and naval plans that it was too late to repudiate this inference…When in 1912 (six years after they had been entered into) Sir Edward Grey communicated these negotiations and arrangements to the Cabinet the majority of its Members were aghast.[3]

In a public speech at the Guildhall on 9 November 1914, British Prime Minister Asquith said that the reason that Britain was fighting was to uphold international law and the rights of small nations. But in the Cabinet the war aims were to uphold the balance of power, which is to say Britain's strategic advantage over her nearest rival: Germany.

One view (historian Christopher Clark's) is that the statesmen of Europe were 'sleepwalkers' going to war by a series of blunders and miscalculations of each other's intentions and the unforeseen consequences of their own. There is something in that account, but you would have to imagine these sleepwalkers as psychotics, all armed with flamethrowers to get the proper effect. The 'accidental war' argument leaves out of account the predisposition to war that is there in those European nations in the summer of 1914, as it had been building up since the later years of the nineteenth century.

Germany's fault

The other explanation for the war is that it was Germany's fault. This is the official view of the war as set down in Article 231 of the Versailles Treaty at the end of the war. Article 231 says:

The Allied and Associated Governments affirm and Germany accepts the responsibility of Germany and her allies for causing all the loss and damage to which the Allied and Associated Governments and their nationals have been subjected as a consequence of the war imposed upon them by the aggression of Germany and her allies.

German leaders were made to sign the Versailles Treaty while their country was under occupation, accepting that they and their allies were responsible for the war. The humiliation of the 'Guilt Clause' and the reparations that Germans were made to pay to the Entente powers kept the hatred of the Great War burning – right up to the Second World War.

French, British and American leaders hung onto the idea that Germany was solely to blame for the war. After the war there were a lot of soldiers and civilians who were angry at the waste of lives. Keeping the finger pointing at Germany was something that the Entente leaders and presses did to stop people asking questions about their own role.

German people hated the humiliation of Versailles. But later generations of German historians, those working after the Second World War, have come to accept that Germany was guilty for what happened in the 1914-18 war.

In 1961 Fritz Fischer's book *Germany's Aims in the First World War* set out the case that Germany had planned domination of Europe and Africa long before the July Crisis – Germany was responsible for the Great War.

Fischer found lots of evidence that senior German officials, generals and politicians had ambitions and even plans for an aggressive forward policy. The imperialist Paul Rohrbach thought that 'whether we shall obtain the necessary territorial elbow room to develop as a world power or not without the use of the old recipe of "blood and iron" is anything but certain' in 1913.[4] When J. K. O'Connor talked to German officers in East Africa in 1913, 'it was evident that the possession of the African continent was the greatest desire of the Teutons'.[5]

Fischer, and the historians who followed him, said that the war was less to do with international conflict ('*Aussenpolitik*') and more to do with what was going on in Germany itself

('*Innenpolitik*'). The war drive and the grab for world power was part of a reactionary social programme to fend off radical challenges. 'Obsessed with the fear of revolution', writes historian Geoff Eley, Wihelmine elites wagered the chances of social cohesion on the prosperity promised by Germany's national strength in the world economy. At the time of the Morocco crisis in 1911 (when the Kaiser challenged French and British predominance there), Rosa Luxemburg wrote that it 'shows again the intimate connection of world policy with the internal political conditions in Germany'. She explained that 'the supreme representation of the German people', the Reichstag, is completely excluded from the most important and momentous events and decisions'.[6] When the war began in 1914 and the Social Democrats repudiated their anti-war position, Kaiser Wilhelm celebrated the end of internal debate: 'I see no parties any more, only Germans.'

The 'Fischer Thesis' about the German war drive is good as far as it goes. For German historians and students trying to understand why their government went to war in 1914 it is very useful. But it is not an explanation of why the war happened, any more than the Guilt Clause in the Versailles Treaty was.

When *Germany's Aims in the First World War* was translated into English it became a different book. It was no longer a book about how the German elite led the country into war. It was a book about how sole responsibility lay with the Germans. But that was not true. Germany did not wage war alone, nor just with her allies Austria and Turkey. The armies of the Entente Powers – Britain, France, Russia and America – after all, were far greater.

Britain's war drive

If we look at what was driving Britain in its decision to wage war, all the features of the warlike German elite are there to be found in the British elite, too. If the war was the fault of the

German leaders, it was the fault of the British leaders, too. The one difference is that the British Empire already dominated the world, whereas the German Empire was still only a plan.

At the start of the twentieth century the British Empire was in deep trouble. The rebellious Boers had risen up in rebellion against British rule, humiliating the British forces and only succumbing militarily after winning the propaganda war against the Empire. Britain was challenged too by the demands for Irish self-government. The Nationalist Party's 2000 strong national convention of 1907 rejected the British Government's modest reforms.

In Britain itself the ruling elite were facing not one but two existential challenges which would change the country forever: the challenge of the unions and the Labour Representation Committee on the one hand, and the challenge of the campaign for Women's Suffrage on the other. The great wave of strikes in the United Kingdom in 1905 and then again in 1911-13 saw the civil authorities close to losing control. At one point the Home Office minister Winston Churchill had battleships anchored off Liverpool, their guns trained at the strike-bound city. At the same time the ruling Liberal Party was dependent on the votes of Members of Parliament who were sponsored by the Labour Representation Committee – as it was also upon the votes of the Irish Nationalist MPs in Parliament. In 1907 Labour candidates took seats from the Liberals in Jarrow and the Colne Valley, signalling a direct challenge to come.

At the same time the Women's Suffrage campaigners kept up a sustained mass campaign of protest, barracking ministers in public, disrupting public meetings, attacking churches, West End shopping arcades and post-boxes. Prime Minister Asquith had a hatchet thrown at him in Dublin and Chancellor David Lloyd George's house was bombed. 'These harpies are quite capable of burning us out,' Winston Churchill wrote to his wife, as he had hundreds jailed and force-fed. Suffragette protestors' civil disobedience jammed the courts, and when jailed they went on hunger strike. British ministers shrunk in horror at the charges of cruelty and cowardice the Suffragettes threw at them at every public meeting.[7]

Faced with all these challenges the ruling British elite struggled to make a convincing case for themselves. Strident imperialism was their most potent public appeal. The Liberal-turned-Unionist Joseph Chamberlain stumped the country whipping up support for 'Tariff Reform' – an appeal to strengthen the ties of Empire and protect British industry against German competition. Agriculture was 'practically destroyed', 'sugar has gone, silk has gone, iron is threatened; the turn of cotton will come', Chamberlain warned. His campaign had the backing of all the big newspapers, the *Daily Mail*, the *Times*, the *Telegraph* and the *Express*. Protecting British industry against foreign competition was a big concern. Books like Williams' *Made in Germany* (1896), Mackenzie's *American Invaders* (1902) and A Shadwell's *Industrial Efficiency* (1906) warned the public of the problem. A *Times* editorial of 1902 warned of 'The Crisis in British Industry'.[8]

Protectionist campaigns against foreign competition also led to racist campaigns against foreign labour. In 1905 the Aliens Act was passed to stop Jewish immigration, at the urging of the British Brothers League and the National Union of Boot and Shoe Operatives. That year there was a great campaign against Chinese labour in South Africa, too. The 'Khaki election' of 1900, just after the Boer War, was won by the Conservatives under Lord Salisbury.

British imperialists like Chamberlain, the historian John Seeley, Secretary of State for the Colonies Sir Alfred Milner, Indian Viceroy Lord Curzon all put the case for a strident defence of the Empire against all enemies, and for government by elites. In the wake of the Boer War, Prime Minister Lord Salisbury complained about the democratic limits on waging war: 'I do not believe in the perfection of the British Constitution as an instrument of war', he said. Salisbury's successor, Balfour, set up the Committee for Imperial Defence in 1902 – replacing the Defence Committee of the Cabinet – to get around the niceties of democratic debate.

The Committee for Imperial Defence aimed to integrate the command of all the armed services of Britain and the colonies – 'the Dominions' must 'realize more fully that their security from attack', said Viscount Esher, 'is inextricably bound up with the security of Britain'.[9] The 'blue water' policy of depending primarily upon naval supremacy was overturned with a commitment to a British Expeditionary Force in Europe; at the same time the committee yoked the navy to its all big-gun capital ship building programme. The Royal Navy War College was set up in 1900, and in 1904 the old commandership-in-chief of the army was replaced with an Army Council. The British Empire was gearing up for war.

The navy's capital ships programme was trumpeted in a great propaganda campaign built around the first of the new battleships, the *Dreadnought*. There was a cult of the *Dreadnought*, which featured in newspapers, magazines, boys' comics and adventure stories. The Admiralty had a full press campaign with booklets and press releases. When the *Dreadnought* visited the Thames in 1909:

> there were chaotic scenes at Southend where the flagship was moored. The main pier to the *Dreadnought* had to be closed again and again because of overcrowding. On the morning of 18 July, an estimated 20,000 people tried to get on to the pier.[10]

'In view of the pan-Germanic aspirations, the British Empire is today confronted by a danger unparalleled in history,' warned military historian C. Stuart Linton.[11] Pro-war journals like

Horatio Bottomley's *John Bull* and Noel Pemberton Billing's *The Imperialist* demanded more Dreadnoughts, and more scholarly journals like the *Commonwealth and Empire Review* were hardly less jingoistic.

Like the German leaders, the British were glad to see that the declaration of war drowned out – temporarily as it happened – the social conflicts that had been tearing the country apart. Lloyd George recorded 'in the course of a single day angry political passions were silenced and followed by the just wrath' of patriotism. Like Germany, Britain's war drive was a response to *'innenpolitik'* – the temptation to silence opposition by cranking up the war drive, and to find a new sense of purpose in war. Suffragettes, Irish Nationalists and trade unionists were, for a while anyway, swallowed up by the great cause of waging war. 'Imperialism is not only a weapon of the ruling class seeking to extend its national domination,' wrote William Paul: 'Imperialism is also a weapon of the capitalist class in its endeavour to prolong class rule and subjugate the proletariat.'[12] The politician who did most to push the war was Winston Churchill, who was Lord of the Admiralty. As gloomy as he had been about the strikers, about the Home Rule crisis and about the social unrest in England, his spirits were raised by the war:

> I love this war. I know it's smashing and shattering the lives of thousands every moment – and yet – I can't help it – I enjoy every second of it.

The arms race and the arms trade

One reason why the Great War has often seemed to have been fated is the arms race. The most arresting side of the arms race was the Naval Arms Race as Germany challenged Britain's monopoly of sea power.

Retiring from Parliament in 1894 the former Prime Minister Gladstone warned that naval expansion was 'the greatest and richest sacrifice ever made on the altar of militarism', and said that, quite apart from the unrestrained spending, 'I dread the effect which the proposals will have on Europe...the peace of Europe.'[13]

In 1900 Kaiser Wilhelm and Admiral von Tirpitz forced through the Fleet Law expanding the German Navy, and soon they were building their own 'Dreadnoughts' – armoured battle ships on the British model. In 1895 the Kaiser had opened the 61-mile-long Kiel Canal opening the way from the naval base on the Baltic Sea to the North Sea, and from 1907 it was widened to make way for the new 'Dreadnought' ships. The socialist leader Karl Liebknecht warned that 'from 1899 to 1906-7 the military budget of Germany alone has grown from about 920 million marks to about 1,300 million, or 40 per cent'. For the workforce, he said, the war drive meant that 'in Germany at present about 655,000 of the strongest and most capable workers, mostly aged between 20 and 22, are withdrawn from work'. He estimated Europe's total military expenditure as equal to 15 per cent of world trade in 1907.[14]

Anyone who cared to step back and think about the Naval Arms Race could see that there was no limit to the vicious circle, and in Parliament Lord Grey warned about 'this tremendous expenditure on and rivalry in armaments'. In the long run it would spiral out of control and 'break civilisation down' – if the cost did not leave us 'bleeding to death in time of peace'. On 21 August 1909 the German Chancellor came up with a proposal to limit the Naval Dreadnought race, a 'Scheme for a general good understanding'. The chief idea was that the Royal Navy would, by agreement, have a built-in superiority in capital ships by the imposition of a ratio of 4:3 in Britain's favour. Not wishing to be cast as the enemy of peace, Grey pretended to 'receive with sympathy any propositions on the part of Germany for an understanding'. But he qualified that by saying that it would have to be 'consistent with the preservation of relations and friendships' with other powers. In private a Foreign Office mandarin noted that 'unless we intend to reverse our foreign policy of preserving the equilibrium in Europe we cannot tie our hands in the manner which Germany proposed to us'. Controlling the arms race was at odds with British power politics.[15]

Looking back at the causes of the Great War in Washington in 1936, the Special Committee on Investigation of the Munitions Industry, under Senator Gerald Nye, concluded that the war had been provoked by arms manufacturers. Arms manufacturers were well-placed to take advantage of the rising war fever.

Alongside the Naval Arms Race was a great boom in the international arms trade led by Krupp, 'Schneider, Skoda, Mitsui, Vickers and Armstrong, Putiloff (Russia), Terni and Ansaldo (Italy), and Bethlehem and Du Pont (America)'. The arms merchants were so wedded to money that it did not matter to them who they armed. In 1906 First Lord of the Admiralty Reginald McKenna asked how it was that Krupp's Kiel shipyards had undertaken to build the Royal Navy eight warships a year.[16]

In 1913 German minister Heeringen protested that, 'it is not the case that I favour private industry', but, 'we are dependent upon it'. Government just could not do what private industry can:

On the other hand we cannot give the private firms enough orders to keep them solvent in peace time. Hence they are dependent on private orders. Who gets the advantage of that? Unquestionably the class they support![17]

That same year Sir John Brunner felt some guilt at the success of his chemical company Brunner, Mond and Co. telling the annual meeting that 'to every sensible man of business the amount of money spent' on national armaments 'must be regarded as a great folly':

These armaments represented an enormous cost to the nations, and the profits accruing from them only went to very few people.[18]

Among the very few to profit were Brunner, Mond and Co., who had an operating profit of £225,000 banked. When the war started net profits climbed from £769,343 in 1914 to £1,117,153 in 1917 – so that they could pay 30 per cent dividend. So, too, did the Bleachers Association's net profits climb from £197,835 in 1915 to £515,583 in 1917.

The British Government raised £3.6 billion in taxes and borrowed a further £7.17 billion to finance the war. Between 1914 and 1920 they spent a massive £11.27 billion – £573 billion in today's money – to spend on explosives, shells, guns, uniforms, transporting and feeding the army.[19]

Nearly half of all the country's output was given over to waging the war, and the government was spending more than half.

The more far-sighted capitalists, like the Minister of Works Sir Alfred Mond, got jobs in the government, organising war production. Mond was John Brunner's partner, and plainly had less of a problem with military spending. Within 3 months of Mond's appointment to the Office of Works:

Seven million pounds were spent on ammunition factories, filling factories and shell stores. Depots costing one million pounds were built, gun and searchlight stations costing a quarter of a million and housing schemes involving almost one million pounds were begun.

'No better business brain has ever been placed at the disposal of the state,' Chancellor and later Prime Minister Lloyd George said: 'we all relied on his great business experience'.[20]

The arms manufacturer Armstrong enjoyed 'the great boom of

wartime activity in which record profits were made', according to the historian of the company, Kenneth Warren:

> In the two months to 14 May 1914, orders for Elswick Ordinance Works totalled £1.1 million; in the two months to 19 November they were already £4.15 million.
>
> Altogether during the war Armstrong produced over 13,000 guns and 12,000 gun mountings. They made 14,500,000 shells, 18,000,000 fuses, 21,000,000 cartridge cases. Their yards built 47 warships and 22 merchant ships. A total of 583 warships were armed...they made 1075 aircraft [up from six before the war] and three airships. They made 100 of the earliest type of tank.[21]

At the end of the war Sir Max Muspratt of the United Alkali Company boasted that 'sulphuric acid is of vital importance to the manufacture of high explosives' and that 'all the resources of the Company were placed freely at the disposal of the Government'. This was, he said, 'a course of action followed patriotically by all the other makers who often sacrificed large profits in their own businesses to meet the national need'.[22] But who was it that sacrificed large profits? Not the United Alkali Company. Their profits ramped up from £193,604 in 1913 to £355,105 in 1915, so that they could pay an 8.5 per cent dividend to their shareholders and put £75,000 into the reserve. By 1918 United Alkali's profits after tax were £384,327 and the dividends on the preference shares bumped up to 10 per cent, and 15 per cent on the ordinary shares.

Sir Max was thrilled:

> Early in 1916 the production was immense, and the vast accumulation of explosives, which made the big victories on the Somme possible, was the direct result of these efforts. Never for a day was an explosive works held up for want of

sulphuric acid.[23]

The 'big victories on the Somme' recall were more than a million casualties, and more than half of those were on the Entente side, without any significant breakthrough.

Ruston Proctor's Lincoln engineering firm saw pre-war profits of £51,928 doubled in the war years. Cortaulds' profits went from £267,669 in 1913 to £1,184,938 in 1918.

'People have come to regard the giving of money for the prosecution of the War...as a profit-making medium', editorialised the *Glasgow Herald* on 27 May 1916. While the *Nation* projected that, 'when the War is over...the propertied people men of this country will be several thousand million pounds the wealthier'. (June 1917) This, recall, when people's living standards were being cut right back. (One business that saw its profits fall was J. Lyons, whose corner-house cafes only prospered when people had money to spend.)

Like British industry, German industry profited greatly from the war. Even before the war Karl Liebknecht pointed out the widespread fraud:

Krupp, Stumm, Ehrhardt, Loewe, Woermann, Tippelkirsch and the corruption that goes with them, the inflated freight and demurrage charges of Woermann, and the net profits of the Powder Ring, amounting to 100 and 150 per cent, which have lightened the German treasury by millions.[24]

Before the war the big chemical concern BASF had doubled its wage bill to 7.88 million marks between 1900 and 1912. BASF's great achievement before the war had been the development of the Haber-Bosch process for nitrogen fertilisers, but in 1914 they turned their attention to a more destructive goal: the German army's desperate need for saltpetre for explosives (which they had previously imported from South America). Promising to synthesise the ingredients – the 'saltpetre promise' – they persuaded the government to pay six million marks for a new plant at Oppau. The firm's capital value jumped from 54 million to 90 million. By 1918, 78 per cent of BASF's 3331 million marks in sales were war related products. 'Synthetic nitrates and ammonia alone accounted for half of sales in 1918.' At their wartime peak, BASF's gross profits stood at 150 million marks, which were ploughed back into the nitrogen plants.[25]

BASF scientist Fritz Haber went to Ypres to supervise the first use of gas in April 1915, using a batch of electrolytic chlorine that was surplus when bleaching was suspended as 'wasteful'. The French and British soldiers were driven out of their trenches to be shot at. Later BASF specialised in more potent poison gases phosgene and diphosgene and eventually mustard gas, which could be made out of by-products from its ammonia plants. Years later BASF's Carl Bosch wondered whether his wartime efforts 'had only extended the war pointlessly and increased its misery'.[26]

Over the course of the war the arms magnate Krupp had made gross profits of 432 million marks. To Gustav Krupp's indignation a former director, Wilhelm Muhlon, wrote in the April 1918 edition of the American magazine *Littell's Living Age* that 'the destiny of the country and the firm are interwoven, and if Germany falls, Krupps and Kruppism will fall with it'.[27]

After the war, US Marine Corps General Major Smedley Butler took to the stump to warn his fellow Americans that 'War is a Racket' – the title of his 1935 booklet, popularising the findings of the Nye Committee. There he points out that the US Government spent $52 billion fighting the war, before going through the record profits that US companies made out of that spending. DuPont (today Dow) averaged profits of $6 million before the war but averaged $58 million making powder for the US Army during the war – 'an increase in profits of more than 950 per cent'. Bethlehem Steel jumped from $6 million earnings before the war to $49m during. United States steel jumped from $105m before the war, to $240m during. The copper company Anaconda earned around $10m a year before the war, but $34m a year during.

> It has been estimated by statisticians and economists and researchers that the war cost your Uncle Sam $52,000,000,000. Of this sum, $39,000,000,000 was expended in the actual war itself. This expenditure yielded $16,000,000,000 in profits. That is how the 21,000 billionaires and millionaires got that way.[28]

Eventually the British Government decided that it would have to recover some of the excess profits its industrialists had made from the war with a special tax. In 1919 the estimate of the country's total excess profits was £3,000,000,000.[29] War profiteers like Sir Max Muspratt complained that their profits would be twice as high if they were not paying the excess. Sir Algernon Frith, President of the Association of Chambers of Commerce, protested that the tax would stop businesses from employing people after the war: 'you are going to cripple us'. Arms manufacturer E. Manville insisted that 'those excess profits are precisely the thing which they have a legitimate right to' – especially as they had to suffer loss of profits in peace time. Patriotic colliery owner Edward Hickman threatened that, 'it will not be worth getting that coal out of the ground, it would be better for it to stop there and wait for better times'. Replying to these 'very genuine' complaints, Treasury Secretary Stanley Baldwin agreed that war profiteers needed incentives, and the duties should not get so high as to take away their initiative.[30]

Employers tried to avoid the excess profits tax. 'Many people had escaped the excess profits duty,' the Liberal politician Herbert Samuel told the Manchester and District Bankers Institute, 'and it was notorious that in spite of it huge sums had been accumulated.'[31]

At the Coal Commission, Inland Revenue inspector Ernest Clarke explained that colliery owners' profits had climbed from £20.3m in 1914 to £50.5m in 1916, an increase in the return on capital from 12.6 per cent to 33 per cent. Still, owners ploughed the cash back into the business, whose capital grew from £135m to £144.5m rather than pay out on dividends, so disguising their profits. By the end of the war the mine owners' profit by the ton was four times as high as before, and their total profits were £160 million.[32]

War profiteering was made possible by the great expenditure by government on munitions, guns and other war materiel. That was a tax on the future, borne by the whole community. But the struggle to hold down the pay and consumption of war workers, outlined before, was the basis for the increased rates of profit. Keeping wages down was the way to make sure that the lion's share of government military spending fell to the employers.

A war for empire

On the eve of the Great War, the British Empire held a territory of 11,900,000 square miles commanding 412 million people, 23 per cent of the world population at the time. Under the agreements that followed – the treaties at Versailles, Sevres and Lausanne – Britain absorbed 1,800,000 square miles and an additional 13 million subjects. The territories of the Ottoman Empire in the Middle East and the German Empire in Africa were shared out between France and Britain. Palestine, Jordan, Iraq, (half of) Cameroon, Togo and Tanganyika all came under her direct rule. Other areas in Africa and the Pacific were granted to the British Dominions of South Africa, Australia and New Zealand. Its territory increased to 13,700,000 square miles – almost a quarter of all land in the world – and those living in its dominions, overseas territories, Crown colonies, protectorates and mandates numbered 460,000,000.

The division of the spoils after the war gives a clue as to the importance of empires in the war.

One of Britain's pressing concerns was control of the oilfields in Basra (the British Navy ran on oil). Before the war Britain could expect that the Turkish governor of Basra would be no threat to the exploitation of oil by Anglo-Persian Petroleum Company and Royal Dutch Shell – to the advantage of Britain. But when Turkey joined the war on the side of the Central Powers the British authorities' determination to control the oil directly came to the fore. They were helped by the overweening ambition of the Government of India (which is to say the British Government of India) to control Mesopotamia. On 6 November 1914 the Anglo-Indian Mesopotamia Expeditionary Force seized the Basra oil fields. The Expeditionary Force's chief political officer, Sir Percy Cox, blithely concluded, 'I don't see how we can well avoid taking over Baghdad.'[33]

On 14 July 1915 Sharif Hussein wrote to Sir Henry McMahon, British High Commissioner in Egypt, asking whether Great Britain would:

recognize the independence of the Arab countries which are bounded: on the north, by the line Mersin-Adana, parallel to 37° N. and thence along the line Krejik-Urfa-Mardin-Midiat-Jazirat (ibn 'Umar') -Amadia to the Persian frontier; on the east, but the Persian frontier down to the Persian Gulf, on the South, by the Indian Ocean (with the exclusion of Aden whose status remains as at present); by the Red Sea and the Mediterranean Sea back to Mersin.

The Sharif was talking about the territory that today is divided between Syria, Iraq, Lebanon, Jordan, Israel, Saudi Arabia, the United Arab Emirates, Bahrain, Qatar, Oman and Yemen.

On 24 October 1915 McMahon wrote to Sharif Hussein, that:

the districts of Mersin and Alexandretta, and portions of Syria lying to the west of the districts of Damascus, Homs, Hama and Aleppo, cannot be said to be purely Arab and must on that account be excepted from the proposed delimitation.

He went on to say that:

I am authorised to give you the following pledges on behalf of the Government of Great Britain: ...subject to the modifications stated above, Great Britain is prepared to recognise and uphold the independence of the Arabs in all the regions lying within the frontiers proposed by the Sharif of Mecca.[34]

On 10 June 1916 the Sharif's forces attacked Turkish troops garrisoned in Mecca. The fighting lasted till the Turks surrendered on 9 July. A force of 3500 tribesmen under the Harb federation led by Sharif Muhsin attacked the Turkish troops at Jedda, who surrendered on 16 June. The Arab Revolt had begun. By 30 September 1917 the Turks withdrew from Damascus in the face of the Arab and British advance, ending 400 years of Ottoman domination. Arab hopes for the post-war settlement were high.[35]

Britain supported the Arab Revolt against the Ottoman Empire

Around the time that Sir Henry McMahon talked to Sharif Hussein, a negotiation between Sir Mark Sykes and M. F. Georges-Picot started at the Foreign Office in London. Picot had been France's consul-general in Beirut. They then went on to Petrograd to talk to the Russian government about the division of the Ottoman Empire after the war. The 'Sykes-Picot' agreement divided Ottoman Arabia between a French and a British sphere of influence. France would dominate in those lands that today are roughly Syria and the Lebanon; Britain in those lands that are Iraq and Jordan. They further stipulated that there would be direct French rule in western Syria and Lebanon, and direct British rule in Basra, Baghdad and the land thereabout. They did concede that there could be a degree of self-government in some parts of these French and British spheres of influence (Zones A and B on their map).

At Russia's request the 'Holy Land' was reserved for an international mandate.[36] On 2 November 1917 the British Foreign Minister Arthur Balfour issued a declaration which committed the government to 'the establishment in Palestine of a national home for the Jewish people'. The Balfour Declaration arose out of discussions with the hard-line imperialists Alfred Milner and Leo Amery, with the Zionist movement leader Chaim Waizmann and British politician Herbert Samuel. Most of all it arose out of a British desire to water down the compelling argument for a single Arab nation.

The Arab leaders' distrust of Britain and France was growing. To derail it the two powers issued an Anglo-French Declaration on 7 November 1918 – 3 days before the end of the war. In it they committed themselves to 'the complete and final liberation of the peoples who have so long been oppressed by the Turks, and the setting up of national governments and administrations that shall derive their authority from the free exercise of the initiative and choice of the indigenous populations'.[37]

Despite their promises, at the end of the war quite a different settlement emerged at the San Remo conference in April 1920 (an extension of the Versailles conference). The Arab lands freed from Ottoman rule were divided between France and Britain roughly along the lines agreed by Sir Mark Sykes and M. Georges-Picot. Under the Versailles terms these were 'Class A Mandates'; that is territories that were governed by Great Powers, on behalf of their peoples who:

> have reached a stage of development where their existence as independent nations can be provisionally recognized subject to the rendering of administrative advice and assistance by a Mandatory until such time as they are able to stand alone.

That meant that they were to be ruled on their behalf for the meantime by Britain or France. France got to govern Syria and Lebanon; Britain got Iraq, Trans-Jordan and Palestine. In Palestine, Britain patronised the small Jewish community. According to Ronald Storrs, who described himself as 'the first military governor of Palestine since Pontius Pilate', Britain would build 'little loyal Jewish Ulster in a sea of potentially hostile Arabism'. The secret committee of Arab officers in the Ottoman Army that had played a key role in the Arab Revolt – *al-'Ahd* – were shocked. They issued a proclamation denouncing the decisions at San Remo and calling on the people of Iraq to resist the dictation of the allied powers by force.[38]

On the other side of the world another carve-up was under way. At the start of the war Germany held a colony in China, Qingdao in Shandong. On 23 August 1914 Japan declared war on Germany and, with the assistance of two British battalions, invaded Qingdao whose German officers surrendered on 7 November. China's contribution of 340,000 labourers to the Entente forces was made in the hope that after the war, China's sovereignty would be honoured. Many of the labourers were recruited from Shandong. China's belief in Woodrow Wilson's promise of 'self-determination', though, was cruelly betrayed. Secretly, the Japanese and Americans had already agreed in the secret Lansing-Ishii Agreement of 1917 to recognise each other's 'interests' in China. At the Versailles Peace Conference China's diplomat Wellington Koo appealed for his country's freedom. But Wilson instead recognised the Japanese colony. On 4 May 1919, in Tiananmen Square, thousands of students and workers protested at the betrayal – 'a new stage in China's bourgeois-democratic revolution against imperialism and feudalism', wrote Mao Zedong 20 years later.

The divisions of China and the former Ottoman Empire between the victorious powers, over the heads of their peoples, was not the only instance of re-division of the imperial spoils. Former German colonies Tanganyika and Cameroon were handed over to Britain and France respectively. South West Africa (today's Namibia) was put into the hands of Britain's Dominion in South Africa, and the African National Congress delegation to the Versailles Peace Conference left empty-handed. In the Pacific the government of the German colony of Samoa was handed over to that other British Dominion, New Zealand. The Mandate system was created to solve a problem:

Namely, how could the Allied powers which had seized (or in the modern jargon 'liberated') German and Turkish dependencies be allowed to keep their gains without affronting people, especially in the United States, who wanted to break free from old-fashioned imperialism?[39]

The imperial share-out had to be dressed up as if it was a matter of 'taking up the white man's burden'.

A war of capitalist competition

When the Great Powers waged war between 1914 and 1918, they were no longer led by chivalric knights, nor fighting for honour.

The war was above all a commercial enterprise. It was fought between rival economic powers who were unable to contain their rivalry. Interior Secretary Clemens von Delbruck dreamt of a German customs union 'from the Pyrenees to Memel, from the Black Sea to the North Sea, from the Mediterranean to the Baltic', saying that 'we are no longer fighting for the master in the internal market but for the mastery in the world market'.[40]

At the end of the war the Entente powers demanded extensive economic reparations from Germany, justified on the grounds that Germany was *guilty*, as established in Article 231 of the Versailles Treaty. According to John Maynard Keynes' biographer, a 'powerful lobby' in Britain pushed the line that Germany must be charged 'the whole costs of the war'. The lobby was made up of 'business interests who wanted German rather than British industry taxed to finance the huge National Debt which the war had created' – meaning the debt contracted boosting their profits – as well as representatives of the Dominions. The original sum demanded was 226 billion Reichsmarks, later reduced to 132 billion, or around £22 billion. Germany did not clear its reparation debts until 2010, when the last payment of £60 million was made. [41]

Entente powers occupied parts of Germany putting them in a position to dictate economic terms. In the French occupied region of the Saar, 'there were not only coal mines but a flourishing metal industry in the control of German magnates. The Saar Government was soon able to "induce" the German magnates to give a 60 per cent participation in their industries to French capital.' *The Worker* saw the pattern emerging:

> Economic compensation, political control to safeguard those economic compensations, and then the further expropriation of the German industrialists.[42]

BASF's Ludwigshafen and Oppau plants were under the French

occupation, which meant that: 'the French utilised the provisions of the Armistice and the Versailles Treaty to study the company's critical production facilities, an apparent case of industrial espionage in the name of arms control'. Under Article 168 of the Versailles Treaty, German factories making war materiel could be closed down unless approved by the victorious powers. 'The French threatened to include BASF's ammonia plants under this provision unless the company licensed the Haber-Bosch technology to them' – that is the process that creates nitrogen fertilisers – which they did under disadvantageous terms.[43] The British chemical giant Brunner Mond did not even bother dealing with BASF, but just announced that they were using confiscated BASF patents licensed to them by the British Government.

BASF was further tasked with making 30,000 tons of ammonia a year for France as reparations. Even as they complained about the yoke of French and British theft of their patents and industrial secrets, the German chemical magnates could find some common ground with their new overlords. The company's management 'found itself depending on French troops to maintain order among striking workers'.

The reparations regime crippled Germany's economy post war, and because Germany was a large market to which many other countries had sold goods it depressed the European and world market too. To keep up reparations payments Germany held down wages, and borrowed the money from creditors, among them the United States, or sought to have the debts rescheduled. It was an arrangement that grossly skewed domestic relations, and Germany's relations with other countries – even destabilising the world financial system and economy. There were different international plans to help Germany meet her obligations. The Dawes Plan of 1924 (US banker Charles Dawes's plan returned the Ruhr Valley, rescheduled debts and extended loans) only postponed the problem, and in 1928 the Young Plan rescheduled again. German governments passed on the cost to their workforces, so that in 1930 in the name of the Young Plan wages were cut:

> The arbitration award in the German metal industry, imposing the very same eight per cent wages cut against which 140,000 Berlin workers struck for three weeks is only the prelude to a new international attack on wages and conditions of the workers in every country in the world.[44]

The whole regime of reparations fostered a poisonous atmosphere in Germany, where foreigners were blamed for the country's privations. The constant sore of reparations and post-war humiliation for Germany was exploited by the emerging nationalist right in the 1930s.

The Great War was often described as the war to end all wars. But the truth was that the way that the war was settled left in place all of the problems that had led to war in the first place. Reactionary political leaders' positions were shored up, exploitative social conditions aggravated, there was an unstable re-division of the colonial world between the powers, militarism was not moderated but enhanced. History would remember the war not as the war to end all wars, nor even as the Great War, but as the First World War, just the prelude to another world war, 20 years later.

Chapter Four

Remembering the War Dead

Eight and a half million soldiers died in the First World War and for the most part they were buried where they fell. In March 1915 Marshall Joffre had ordered that no bodies could be dug up. Some British soldiers' bodies were repatriated. But that was on an *ad hoc* basis without a general rule. In practice that meant that officers whose families had influence were more likely to be repatriated while most were left where they were first buried. One of the last bodies to be brought back was that of Lieutenant William Gladstone, a Member of Parliament since 1911, and the grandson of the former Prime Minister William Gladstone.

In 1916 Sir Fabian Ware got the Adjutant General to ban all further exhumations and repatriations. From then on, the rule was that no bodies were to be brought back, but to be left where they were buried in northern France, Belgium or the other makeshift war graves.

The reason for the ban was explained in different ways. Marshall Joffre said that it was a health hazard. Red Cross leader Sir Fabian Ware was worried that the *ad hoc* repatriations would show that officers and men were not equal in death. Behind all of these claims was the fact that the British Army, like other armies in the combat, would not commit themselves to a general rule of bringing the bodies back. It was not possible, they thought, because of the logistical commitment, because of the cost, and because the mass repatriation of bodies would undermine morale, in the army and at home.

At the end of the war the British Government faced a dilemma. The grieving families had no body to bury. Their sons had given up their lives to the British Empire, but they would not even have a grave they could tend. Feelings were running high, and the government appointed an Imperial War Graves Commission to manage the problem.

The War Graves Commission decided that the rule that bodies would not be brought back should hold after the war. The commission was 'aware of a strong desire…that exhumations should be permitted'. But they dismissed that with the argument that 'it would be contrary to the principle of equality of treatment', meaning that the *ad hoc* repatriations would favour the wealthy. In fact most of the bodies were exhumed, but only so that they could be reburied in tidy lines in France and Belgium.[1]

Though they were painted as selfish rich people, those who wanted their sons brought back were not. Around 90 letters a week landed in the War Graves Commission's post box asking for repatriation.[2] In 1919 the British War Graves Association was formed by Sarah Ann Smith, whose son Frederick was buried in the Grevillers Cemetery at the Somme. The association, which grew to around 15,000 strong, mostly in the north, wanted the return of the war dead to England. William Dawson had visited his son Robert in hospital in France, but when the soldier died of his wounds, William was not allowed to take his son's body back. Dawson wrote to the War Graves Commission quoting the Versailles Treaty, that said that signatories would offer 'every facility for giving effect to requests that the bodies of the soldiers and sailors may be transferred to their own country' – but they did not budge.

Ruth Jervis wrote to the commission asking: 'is it not enough to have our boys dragged from us and butchered (and not allowed to say 'nay') without being deprived of their poor remains?' In a second letter she protested, 'the country took him, and the country should bring him back'.[3]

The one option that the War Graves Commission never looked at was that the army should bring all the bodies back. The costs – financially and to morale – were just too high. The cost of sending the men to the front was a necessary one, but the cost of bringing them back was not to be considered.[4] In 1924 Prime Minister Ramsay MacDonald wrote an abrupt letter to Sarah Ann Smith of the British War Graves Association saying that it would be impossible to move 800,000 bodies 'scattered all over the world'.[5]

As well as barring repatriation, the War Graves Commission decided that all graves should follow a uniform style. This was too much for some of the bereaved, who wanted to put their own headstones on their sons' graves. In the House of Lords 'an unexpectedly strong current of opposition' to the policy was voiced, calling it a 'gross and wicked tyranny'.[6]

The Chinese Labour Corps were made to stay on after the war to clear the battlefields

What few people were willing to admit was that a great many of the markers that were in place did not correspond to the bones beneath them. At the end of the war there were to be 580,000 identified and 180,000 unidentified graves, and 530,000 men whose graves were not known. 'Soldiers returning wounded or on leave to England were complaining bitterly,' warned Fabian Ware in 1917, 'about the number of bodies still lying out on the

Somme battlefield'. Edward Lutyens, the architect who designed the cemeteries, found the sites in 'disarray', 'a ribbon of isolated graves like a milky way across miles of country, where men were tucked in where they fell'. Among those clearing up the battlefield were the Chinese Labour Corps, under slave-like conditions. Where the graves were gathered in larger groups, Lutyens worried that they were packed so close together that it would be hard 'to arrange their names in decent order'. (Lutyens liked an orderly display and he took great pride in laying the graves out in endless rows, as if the bodies were still on parade.)[7]

The 250,000 Africans who lost their lives in the service of the British Army were treated even worse. The British governor of Tanganyika territory told the War Graves Commission that he 'considered that the vast Carrier Corps Cemeteries at Dar es Salaam and elsewhere should be allowed to revert to nature as speedily as possible'.[8] There is a generic bronze monument to native forces, including the Carrier Corp, at Mwembe Tiyari in Mombasa, but the war grave at Dar es Salaam lists only 1843 dead, mostly European soldiers and some of the King's African Rifles. Where there were war memorials put up for non-white troops, as for the Indian Army losses in Mesopotamia, the Nigerian Regiment and the West African Frontier Force, only the officers' names were engraved in stone.[9] An official history of the War Graves Commission regretted that 'the traditions of the Indian Army... paid great attention to the graves of expatriate Britons but little to those of Indian servicemen'. So it was that 'by 1924 every British grave had a headstone, but nothing had been done to commemorate the Indians', and when extra funds were released to set about that 'it was too little and too late'.[10] The Nigerian forces monument put up in 1932 in Lagos did honour the Carrier Corps along with the Hausa Regiment, but it did not carry the names of the African dead of the Great War until 2015, when it was relocated to the new cemetery at Abuja and more than 2000 names from both world wars were added.

The decision not to return the bodies of the dead troops to their grieving families left an emotional hole that had to be filled. Instead of being mourned by their loved ones individually, the dead were to be dragooned into a collective commemoration. Official commemoration of the dead would take the families' grief and turn it into a collective worship of the war dead, making them a sacrifice to the God of War – or more prosaically, to King George, General Haig and the other chieftains who had sent the men off to be killed in the first place.

The case against war had been strongly put. The best argument against the war was the cost in lives. What the official commemoration of the dead did was to take all the grief that might have counted against the war-mongers and turn it instead into part of the case for war. The dead were now called the 'fallen' (though most had been struck down). The killing was sanctified as a 'sacrifice' – the 'Greatest Sacrifice'. 'Scarcely a British family was untouched in some way or degree by the war: to hundreds of thousands came the greatest sacrifice of all', editorialised the *Daily Mail* on 11 November 1919. They had been sacrificed to the greater glory of the British Empire. At the first official Remembrance Day, Prime Minister David Lloyd George laid a wreath with his own hand-written note: 'A token of gratitude to those who died that we might live more abundantly'.[11] It was true that British industrialists enjoyed a massive increase in profits in the war, and Lloyd George like most British statesmen had investments that paid good dividends. But for most of the ex-soldiers and ordinary men and women of Britain, the years after the war were not ones of abundance, but of more 'sacrifice'.

Remembrance Day

On the day of the Armistice marking the end of the war, 11 November 1919, most people were just glad it was over. 'There was no sense of victory, much less any hatred of the enemy,' recalled Captain Alan Thomas of the 6th Battalion, 'only a strong desire to get home'. In London and other English towns, the crowds celebrated through the night, but diaries and letters of the time show that many who had lost loved ones were privately grieving while the world cheered. Daisy Davies' daughter remembered that her mother had borne the death of her husband Charles stoically, and was surprised to find her weeping over the washing on Armistice Day. 'Well, I have no one to come home and love me,' her mum explained.[12]

There were celebrations, but they did not last. Many soldiers were angry that they could not go home straight away. Marooned in demobilisation camps, waiting for trains and ferries, the men rioted. On 3 January 1919 British soldiers who were in Britain on Christmas leave were ordered to return to the continent. When they gathered at Dover and Folkestone, 9000 of them refused to get on the boats. On 4 and 5 March, Canadian soldiers in the Kinmel Camp in Wales broke out. Three of the rioters and two sentries were killed as it was put down, and 21 injured. All told around 50,000 soldiers took part in protests demanding repatriation. Also, as the No-Conscription Fellowship pointed out, '1,600 Conscientious Objectors are still in prison' – many of them for their second year.[13] With one eye on the mutinies of German, Russian and French servicemen, the authorities in Britain were fearful. Sir Basil Thompson, the Special Branch Metropolitan Police Commissioner, said that 'during the first three months of 1919 unrest touched its high watermark', and, 'I do not think at any time in history since the Bristol Riots we have been so near to revolution'.

Official ceremonies and parades, and the building of monuments, played an important part in restoring order. The Cenotaph, Edward Lutyens' monument to the war dead, was first unveiled not at 'Remembrance Day' – the anniversary of the Armistice in November – but at a Victory Parade in July – 'Joy Day'. At the procession, Butcher Haig saluted the bust of Lord Kitchener. 'The hosts of the dead,' wrote the *Manchester*

Guardian's reporter, 'were commemorated in the simple classical Cenotaph, tall and narrow and white.' Sir Edward Lutyens' Cenotaph of July 1919 was a temporary structure, made of plaster and wood, like a Hollywood set piece, that 'had risen in a day out of Whitehall'.[14]

On the same day, a different assembly was held in Merthyr Tydfil, where 25,000 gathered to remember the dead, but also to demand higher pensions for ex-servicemen and their dependents. In Luton, ex-servicemen were told they could not hold their own commemoration – so they set fire to the town hall, and when the firemen turned up the soldiers held them back until the building was gutted. Luton was put under martial law for several days. In Chertsey, servicemen boycotted the victory parade, protesting over pensions, as well as the sending of the British Expeditionary Force to Russia, to attack the fledgling Soviet Union.[15]

James Cox, President, International Union of Ex-Service Men, said:

> the whole thing is a mockery, and it is sheer hypocrisy to ask the discharged men to take part in what is officially termed 'joy day,' while the widows and dependents of his fallen comrades are housed in hovels and existing in a state of semi-starvation.[16]

James Cox could see how the armed services were being used to put down protests by working people after the war, like those in Glasgow and Belfast. 'Just as their army and navy was used to defend their economic interests abroad,' labour activist William Paul wrote, 'so now are the armed forces to be used to defend the economic interests of the financiers at home.'[17]

There were some doubts among traditionalists about the Cenotaph. The *Church Times* saw 'a cult' of 'Cenotapholotry' and the *Catholic Herald* thought it was 'Pagan'. Lord Alfred Mond thought it was maudlin and defeatist, and wanted it taken down after the Victory Parade. But the government needed to keep its grip on the way that the dead were remembered to make sure that they were not recruited to more radical causes, like proper pensions for ex-servicemen, or worse, against the intervention in Russia. The Cenotaph was kept up for the first anniversary of the Armistice, which was the first Remembrance Day, on 11 November 1919. On the order of the King, 'there was made a great silence', reported the *Daily Mail:*

> The King was right. His minutes of silence were golden, with memory and hope and new faith that the torch received 'from dying hands at Flanders fields' will be carried on.[18]

The crowds were large, and French Premier Clemenceau joined Lloyd George at the ceremony. Across the country, reported the *Daily Mail,* people stopped in silence: 'mill girls cried when the looms were stopped'; in the Nottingham Assizes Court, ex-soldier Frederick Carter stood for 2 minutes' silence after the King's Letter was read to the court – before he was sentenced to death by Mr Justice Greer for killing his landlady.

Once again there were protests of unemployed veterans who had to be kept back, and in Manchester a representative of the Ex-Servicemen's Association was refused permission to address the procession there on 'the case for the living, in honour of the dead'. The British War Graves Association held a mass rally calling for repatriation of the bodies the night before. Ex-Servicemen's leader James Cox wrote that it would have been better to reflect 'on how the widows and dependents of the fallen are being treated, and to what treatment the maimed and disabled men are being subjected to since their return to civil life'.[19]

Lutyens' wood and plaster structure was looking tatty, and the Ministry of Works announced that it would come down in

January 1920. But the *Daily Mail* and other newspapers started up a campaign for a permanent Cenotaph – which was unveiled by King George in November 1920: 'The Cenotaph, its new Portland stone a pale lemon, rose before us naked and beautiful', the *Manchester Guardian* trilled.[20]

The word 'Cenotaph' means an empty coffin or tomb. Sir Edward's design for the Cenotaph at Whitehall is clearly a coffin, or sarcophagus, set high on a great pedestal that soars above the crowds. In keeping with the Art Deco style, Lutyens' Cenotaph is spare but with non-classical proportions, many times higher than it is long or broad, like a Charles Rennie Mackintosh chair back. It has no explicit religious symbols (which is what irritated the churches). The inscriptions read, 'the Glorious Dead', and '1914-1918'. The meaning of Lutyens' Cenotaph is that the empty coffin stands in for the war dead, who were left on the battlefield. It is a substitute for personal grief, redirected into a public ceremony. This was how the abandonment of the dead in Flanders and northern France was to be justified – with a token tomb in place of a real one.

The Unknown Soldier

To add to the meaning, the unveiling of the new Cenotaph was coupled with the burial of an 'Unknown Soldier' in Westminster Cathedral. The idea was that:

> The burial of an unknown fighting man among the great men of history with impressive pageantry will express the honour the nation pays to the legions of fighting men who fell, whose sacrifice is commemorated in another way in the Cenotaph.

Like the Cenotaph, the price of fame was anonymity. The soldier would always remain unknown to earn his place among 'the great men of history': 'Whether a soldier or an airman, a man of Great Britain or the Dominions, will never be known.'[21] He could be anyone, that is, as long as he was British, or from one of Britain's white colonies (Canada, New Zealand, Australia, Newfoundland or South Africa – which only sent white troops).

The British Cabinet read a paper that October that said that 'it would do honour to the great mass of fighting men'. They resolved that 'the remains of one of the numerous unknown men who fell and were buried in France should be exhumed' to be reburied in Westminster Abbey, the 'symbolic exception' to the rule that no soldier was to be disinterred and repatriated.[22]

The Cenotaph, as seen by Arthur Wragg for the Peace Pledge Union

The Unknown Soldier, like the empty sarcophagus in Whitehall, would always remain a lifeless abstraction, while real, living ex-servicemen and the bereaved relatives were left to look on, spectators at their own symbolic interment.

'With honours and devotion passing those given to Kings, the nameless warrior was buried in Westminster Abbey yesterday,' reported the *Manchester Guardian*: 'The body of the unknown, brought in procession from Victoria Station, reached the Cenotaph' just as the King unveiled it and Big Ben struck 11. The *Times* editorialised that the Unknown Soldier was 'the silent ambassador of the legion dead to the courts of the living', and was 'an emblem of the "plain man", of the masses of the people who in every age, have borne their full share of our national wars'. That month the International Federation of Trades Unions took a different view declaring 'that the fight against militarism and war, and for world peace, based on the fraternisation of the people, is one of the principle tasks of the unions'.[23]

The poets were sceptical of the official celebrations. Auden wrote:

> Let us honour if we can
> The vertical man
> Though we value none
> But the horizontal one.

Siegfried Sassoon imagined one visitor:

> The Prince of Darkness to the Cenotaph
> Bowed. As he walked away I heard him laugh.

With that, the Remembrance Day commemoration became part of Britain's official, secular ceremonial.

Later Remembrance Days

On 11 November 1921 the *Daily Herald* published a poem by George Slocombe, *The Phantom Army*. Slocombe imagined the ghosts of the Great War marching up Whitehall: 'An army of dead men, and marching before/Harry of Hackney, Commander-in-Chief.' 'Harry whom Hackney will see no more' marches into Downing Street and sits in the Prime Minister's seat writing Royal Proclamations on a pad 'to the poor People of this Here Land': 'work for the workless' and 'bread for the starving'. When the Prime Minister finds the notepad he pushes it away: 'The dead are dead, thank God! And they will never come back.' 'But woe for him,' wrote Slocombe, 'if the dead came back.'

On 11 November 1921 the Clyde Workers' Committee newspaper, *The Worker*, led with a cartoon by Chas Boyle, the Old Contemptibles, with death standing alongside a top-hatted capitalist embraced by death at the top of a pile of skulls. Death thanks the capitalist for his 'magnificent achievements in my service'. The capitalist replies 'pooh! A mere bagatelle to what I

The "Old Contemptibles."

am going to do the next war for freedom.'

Alongside the cartoon, *The Worker* carried a poem by the radical politician Henry Labouchere, as an antidote to the imperial propaganda of the Remembrance Day Parade:

Where is the flag of England?
Seek the land where the natives rot.

And decay and assured extinction
Must soon be the people's lot.
Go to the once fair islands
Where disease and death are rife,
And the greed of a callous commerce
Now battens on human life.
Where is the flag of England?
Go sail where rich galleons come
With their shoddy and loaded cotton,
And beer and Bibles and rum.
Seek the land where brute force hath triumphed
And hypocrisy hath its lair,
And your question will thus be answered —
For the flag of England is there.

In the lead up to the Remembrance Day parade *The Worker* reported that 'throughout the length and breadth of Britain great demonstrations are being organised to declare – Never Again!'

Disillusioned and weary, disgusted and fed up with the aftermath of the Imperialist bloodbath of 1914-18, the masses are rising to declare, 'There shall be no imperialist wars.'[24]

The Worker was focused on the British actions against Turkey. Under the headline 'War! What For?' they warned that 'the Imperialists of Britain are preparing another massacre of the working class', and 'their kept Press is commencing to beat the War Drum'. British claims to stand for 'the Freedom of the Seas' was 'a joke in the mouths of representatives of the power which controls the sea-trade routes throughout the world'. *The Worker* was sharply critical of the war-mongers' claim that the action was called so 'that the gains of the late war shall not be lost'.

The late war had no gains for the workers. The heroes who

fought in it are all at the starvation level now, whether employed or unemployed. The unemployed serviceman is batoned ruthlessly should he try to manifest his independence. The disabled ex-serviceman is kicked from pillar to post.[25]

There was precious little reason to put faith in the peace negotiations to limit arms. Listen to Field Marshall Sir William Robertson, cautioned *The Worker:*

We should disregard all pious aspirations and shams regarding international agreement for limiting or prohibiting aerial warfare. Agreement or no agreement, when a nation has its back to the wall, it will, and ought to, use every means for bursting its adversary.[26]

In September 1923 the National Peace Council organised 70 demonstrations all over the country under the 'No More War' slogan.[27] That November *The Worker* headlined 'Watch War-Mongers Hypocrisy on Armistice Day'. 'Their name liveth for evermore', wondered *The Worker,* or 'should it be "forgotten already"?'

The fifth anniversary of the world war finds the Capitalist States of the world reeling through poverty and famine towards a fresh imperialist massacre.[28]

Enemies of war in 1923 were horrified by the punitive reparations that the allies had imposed upon defeated Germany. The National Peace Council warned that 'the fate not only of millions of our fellow human beings but the future peace of the world becomes more precarious every day'.[29]

'I have never seen anything so dreadful in all my experience,' Ruth Fry of the Friends War Victims' Relief Committee told the *Manchester Guardian* after visiting the Ruhr:

No one has any coal. Hot meals are an impossibility. The people are living on bread and margarine.[30]

In 1924 the National Peace Council again held demonstrations on the 'No More War' theme, this time in 152 cities and towns, and followed those up with a national 'No More War' conference. Two thousand turned up for a meeting at the Holborn Empire. The National Peace Council also held an Emergency Meeting on the Egyptian Crisis at Essex Hall, on 2 December, after British officers massacred villagers. Philip Snowden argued that 'a dreadful murder had been committed, a crime which should not be condoned by partial silence'. Other speakers were George Lansbury and Captain Wedgwood Benn.[31]

In 1928, in Parliament anti-war MPs challenged the government's commitment to disarmament. Labour MP Rennie Smith asked the Secretary of State for Air about the air display at Hendon: 'Is the Minister going to have a display of the bombing of a native village, as was the case last year?'

Samuel Hoare said that there would be a set piece but 'the bombing will not be of a native village'. 'Will it be a civilised village this year?' asked Lt-Commander Kenworthy. At that MPs suggested 'a replica of the House of Commons', 'with dummy Minister'. In the programme for the 1930 Hendon Air Display the 'native tribesmen' were re-named 'international outlaws', but the meaning, as the National Peace Council pointed out, was the same: the Royal Air Force had perfected the aerial bombardment of 'native villages' in Iraq between 1920 and 1924.[32]

Since there was a Labour government in power, peace protestors hoped that they could get them to turn away from war. Dr Alfred Salter asked Labour War Minister Tom Shaw if the Armistice Day could be turned into a peace and memorial service:

Impossible! Unthinkable! It would be opposed by the highest

authorities!.

Why! We get more recruits for the Army in the fortnight following the Armistice ceremony than in any other time of year![33]

In 1931 the peace movement was having an impact on the establishment's ownership of Great War Remembrance. Nearly six thousand people went to a rally on Armistice Eve at the Albert Hall, with George Lansbury and Richard Sheppard speaking on No More War. The Women's International League's disarmament petition had 1.5 million signatures.[34]

In 1937 campaigners argued that 'Armistice Day can be used for peace'. The official celebrations were 'to make use of it, by association, to strengthen the war convention': 'There will be the poppies with their sentimental association with picturesque battlefields, instead of the reality of war.' The 'innumerable memorials up and down the country' suggest 'that heroes laid down their lives, instead of got the death they were giving others'. The peace activists were planning an outdoor meeting with the MP Isaac Foot, the novelist Storm Jameson and Canon Dick Sheppard in Regent's Park on Armistice Day.[35] Meanwhile other campaigners were planning 'a substitution for, or counteraction of, the red poppy' by selling white poppies, to raise money for War Resisters' International, and for conscientious objectors in prison all over the world.

'Year by year a greater proportion of the nation becomes tired of the military preparations held in regard to the so-called "War to end war",' said the General Secretary of the Women's Cooperative Guild, calling on all to wear the white poppy. The Peace Pledge Union's supporters planned to tackle sellers of the Haig Fund's red poppies 'to challenge the seller as to what she is doing to prevent war'.

They took risks, arguing with the Haig Fund's red poppy sellers. Two clerks were sacked from their jobs for wearing the white poppy to work, told that it was 'an absolute insult to the company'.[36]

When Remembrance Day was cancelled

In 1937 an editorial in *Peace News* asked, 'what if a greater tragedy should occur? Would that obliterate this celebration?' A Canadian veteran made a similar point that 'another war would make a mockery of the solemn remembrance of the dead'.[37]

Artist E. E. Briscoe imagined a bombed Cenotaph in *Peace News* in 1937

Two years later, Europe was once again at war. What happened to Remembrance Day then?

In 1939 the government announced that, 'The ceremony at the Cenotaph will not be held as there is a danger that the sound of the sirens may be thought to be warning of an air raid.' In *Peace News* John Barclay wrote, 'the grim irony of this bald official statement needs no comment'.[38]

10 November 1940 was the 'Strangest Day of Remembrance' according to the *Daily Mail*. At St Paul's 'two thousand people usually attend this service', but 'yesterday there were only 80'.

> Armistice Sunday usually sees a great throng of sightseers and pilgrims...But yesterday they only came in small groups, singly, in couples...ex-Service men and women, all of them wearing a badge of service in the present struggle.
>
> Four middle aged men placed a large wreath of Flanders' Poppies at the foot of the monument...Occasionally there were passers-by...

The following year, the Bishop of Chelmsford wrote:

> Today is Armistice Day. There will be no official observance and no organised ceremonial. But these things are not indispensable: we can each keep our Two-Minutes Silence in our own way and we shall do.

The bishop promised that the parents of the dead 'will flush with pride as they greet their hero children in the Great Beyond'.[39]

The *Daily Mail*, the paper that campaigned to have a permanent Cenotaph, carried a cartoon by Illingworth, applauding the decision to abandon the Remembrance Day parade and the two minutes' silence.

'No nation-wide silence stilled Britain yesterday – the 23rd anniversary of the 1918 Armistice,' reported the *Daily Mail* on 12

Illingworth's cartoon for the *Daily Mail*

November 1941: 'Arms factories, dockers, shipbuilders, miners carried on the drive for final victory.'

Not everyone had got the government memo that grief was suspended for the duration: 'many gathered at the Cenotaph in Whitehall to pay private homage as traffic rattling by dulled the tones of Big Ben striking eleven'.

> Women, carrying shopping bags, hurried between traffic streams to lay their humble tributes.

The meaning of Remembrance Sunday was that it squared the circle, connecting the grief and unhappiness of the war with the case for the military. Grief was repackaged as 'sacrifice'. Militarism was dressed up as 'honouring the dead'. The great upsurge of anger at the human cost of the war was acknowledged by those that sent the men to their deaths, then it was twisted and turned until it could be redirected into a solemn adoration of the God of War.

Anzac Day

Australia and New Zealand have their own commemoration day, 'Anzac Day', for the Australian and New Zealand Army Corps, on 25 April. The date is that of the opening of the Battle of Gallipoli, when 65,000 'Anzacs' joined the Entente force that took on the Ottoman troops under Mustafa Kemal. Eight thousand, seven hundred and nine Australians were killed at Gallipoli and 2721 New Zealanders. The first commemoration of Anzac Day was the following year, 1916, in many towns in Australia and New Zealand. Since 1920 Anzac Day has been an official holiday in New Zealand, and since 1921 in Australia, to commemorate the 60,000 Australians and 18,000 New Zealanders who were killed in the war.

But while Australians and New Zealanders remembered the sacrifice of their young men, the commemoration was intermingled with bitterness towards Britain and the Entente war-mongers.

The main flaw in the Gallipoli landing was that it left the troops stuck on a narrow beach, below a great cliff, from which Mustafa Kemal's forces could bombard them at will. Churchill – as so often – was carried away with the idea of a *coup de grace* that would hand him the war in a single stroke. It was a piece of magical thinking brought on by the intractability of the Western Front, but it turned out to be a terrible human sacrifice to Churchill's folly. Admiral John Fisher wrote to Churchill warning him that his plan would lead to disaster: 'you are bent on forcing the Dardanelles and nothing will turn you from it – nothing'.[40] Worse still, Churchill made sure that Fisher's doubts were kept from the Cabinet. In 1917 the Dardanelles Royal Commission reported that the First Lord of the Admiralty, Churchill, was 'carried away' by 'his sanguine temperament and his firm belief in the success of the undertaking which he advocated'.

The 1917 report condemned Lord Kitchener, too, finding that he was unable to delegate, leading to 'confusion and want of efficiency', that because of him there was no meeting of the War Council between 19 March and 14 May 1915, and that Kitchener 'held back additional troops for three weeks without telling Churchill'. Peace activist Len Fox, who wrote a pamphlet *The Truth About ANZAC* in 1937, concluded that 'these were the two men who led the Anzacs to their death – an over-imaginative politician and an under-imaginative general, who blundered on as their fancy dictated, without and even against the advice of experts, and even of each other'.[41]

Faces of the men of the Anzac as they approached the shore

The misery of the men pinned on the beach was made worse by the military's failure to supply them with water so that 'several men went raving mad with thirst'. More, 'the provision for the evacuation of the wounded', admitted the commission, 'proved insufficient'.[42] On 11 March 1926 Labour MP Hugh Dalton pointed out that the Turkish Army was firing on the men below the cliff with armaments supplied by the British firm Vickers. He asked the House of Commons:

Did it matter to the directors of these armament firms, so long as they did business and expanded the defence expenditure of Turkey, that their weapons mashed into a bloody pulp all the morning glory that was the flower of Anzac, the youth of Australia and New Zealand, yes, and the youth of our own country?

Anzac Day was important to Australia and New Zealand's ruling elites. But for the ordinary people it always had a different meaning, since it stood for the way that they had been treated as cannon fodder by the Westminster government. The radical historian James Rawling wrote in 1937: 'Anzac Day commemorates one of the foulest crimes that has ever been committed against the working class of this country', and yet 'thousands still surround the day with dreams of glory and accolades of honour'. Still, Rawling was confident that 'once the masses of Australia understand fully the horror of that crime at Anzac, the obscenity of the offering to God Capital, then their indignation will be so much greater for all the bombast and talk of glory that surround its celebrations'.[43]

Rawling was prophetic. In the 1970s and 1980s, anti-war and feminist protestors took their cause to the Anzac Day Parade. So scandalised was the Australian Government that anyone should be off-script that they decided to 'make it an offence for persons to disrupt an Anzac Day Parade or an observance or ceremony at or near the Australian War Memorial'.[44] In 1981 peace protestor Lyn Lenox was prosecuted, but the jury would not convict.

Chapter Five

Ireland and the Poppy

British governments have tried hard over the years to present the role of British soldiers in Ireland as that of peacekeepers, but that is not how most Irish people have seen it. They have viewed the British military as occupiers and oppressors. At best they have perceived the British Army as part of the problem rather than as part of the solution. As Irish commentator Fintan O'Toole put it, 'the army had been a player not a referee'.[1] Though no friend of Irish republicanism, O'Toole says the British troops in Northern Ireland made things worse: 'the army did more to feed the flames than quench them'. In the eyes of British soldiers anyone opposed to British rule was an enemy. Soldiers arrived with a colonial mentality in the 1970s seeing Northern Ireland as another field for the operations it had run in Malaysia, Kenya, Aden and Cyprus, identifying Catholics as a suspect population. Most people killed by soldiers were innocent civilians not armed combatants. In many instances military leaders attempted to cover up and deny such killings. Helped by a compliant British media, a common tactic was to lie and pin the blame on the IRA. It has taken years of exhaustive campaigning by families and communities to expose the full truth and scale of killings before military leaders and governments have accepted responsibility. In many instances they still refuse to own up to their actions. They continue to block families in their attempts to reveal the full circumstances of their loved ones' murders at the hands of soldiers. In this context and with this history it should come as no surprise that the red poppy commemorating British soldiers evokes not admiration but contempt in parts of Ireland.

Sometimes military leaders are refreshingly honest when assessing the role of troops during the Troubles. General Sir

Mike Jackson wrote that 'it could be argued that the army did make the situation worse by, in practice, alienating the Catholic community...a desire to "sort the Micks out" was often apparent'.[2] Gus Hales, a soldier who saw tours of duty in North Belfast and South Armagh, explained how his fellow soldiers saw all Catholics and Nationalists as the enemy. He recalled how they harassed, intimidated and generally made life difficult for local nationalists.[3] Malachi O'Doherty, a Belfast journalist, described the kind of experience growing up in nationalist West Belfast that is too insignificant to make the history books, but which was a typical experience for thousands. The back door of his house was kicked in and he was dragged out into the garden by a soldier who threatened to shoot him.[4] Fortunately, he was only kicked and beaten. Not far from where O'Doherty lived, Joan Connolly was one of ten victims killed in Ballymurphy, West Belfast, over several days in 1971 by the British Parachute Regiment. She was shot several times in the head and body. Eye witnesses claim soldiers refused emergency medical attention as she cried out for help. This mother of eight bled to death.[5]

There were many good young men in the British Army sent to the north of Ireland. The majority of them had no real understanding of what they were signing up for. They were mostly young lads from working-class communities and straight out of school. Before they knew it, they were in uniform, a rifle in hand and being jeered and resented by the very population their political masters had told them they were going to Ireland to help. Tragically, and too often, their initial naivety and optimism morphed into a desire 'to sort the Micks out'. According to Nottingham University professor Edward Burke, recruits to British Army regiments became 'hyper-invested' in its traditions and honour to the exclusion of democratic norms.[6]

An example of this 'regimental tribe' mentality is illustrated by the double murder of two farm workers in Fermanagh – Michael Nann and Andrew Murray. Both were knifed to death by soldiers of the Argyle and Sutherland Highlanders in an operation whose purpose has remained obscure, not least because there was no investigation of the incident until seven years later when an army sergeant admitted to the murder. There was no evidence whatever to indicate either man was in the IRA but Nann had previously been involved in the civil rights movement and was a nationalist. This was enough to sign his death warrant. Soldiers approached the farm. The sergeant confronted Michael Nann in his byre and knifed him in the stomach. After Nann 'died on me' the sergeant reported, he went out and, with the help of his men, stabbed Michael Murray, who had been forced to lie on the ground, with the same knife.[7]

Were the four soldiers involved in these murders just 'rotten apples' in an otherwise healthy barrel? The evidence points to the contrary: they were socialised into this type of behaviour by their military superiors in accordance with the regimental ethos. For example, Sergeant Hathaway who led the murder gang had been an exemplary soldier, a stickler for the rules. It was not his personal character but the character of his 'tribe' that explains this atrocity. On top of the obsessional self-regard cultivated by most British Army regiments, the Argyles had developed a self-image as 'players', hard men, who enjoyed 'welting people over the head'. Many of these particular soldiers had been commanded by Colin 'Mad Mitch' Mitchell in Aden where they learned the habit of casual brutality.

History records that Britain's military presence anywhere in the world has brought with it atrocities and suffering for the local population. Ireland was no different whether it was at the time of the Irish War of Independence (1918-21) or the Troubles in the north (1969-2007) – the legacy was a bloody one. During the recent conflict military intelligence engaged in a practice pioneered in other colonial conflicts of getting local 'players' to do the killing for them. They either manipulated, directed or created loyalist murder gangs to do their dirty work. In a minority of cases IRA members would be targeted but for the most part it involved assassination of innocent Catholics. The 'Glenanne gang' was one such murder squad. They carried out around 120 killings. Catholic farmers, shopkeepers, publicans and businessmen were slaughtered in a bloody decade of bombings and shootings in the counties of Tyrone and Armagh.[8]

For years local people claimed that scores of these murders were carried out by loyalist paramilitary gangs, actively guided and helped by the Royal Ulster Constabulary and the British Army, in particular the Ulster Defence Regiment. The evidence detailing over 100 of these murders has now been documented in gruesome detail. This was not just a case of a few bad apples or rogue British military involved. The highest ranks in British military and intelligence were complicit and knew the extent of British security forces involvement.[9]

The lived experience and price of British loyalist collusion means many in Ireland associate the red poppy not with honour and self-sacrifice of British soldiers but collusion in the murder of Catholics. Debates about the emblem continue to provoke anger and tension.[10] In the hamlets, towns and counties of the north nationalist residents reject the poppy by reciting the lists of dead from their area murdered by British soldiers or their allies. In South Armagh they recount how on a bright summer's day 12-year old Majella O'Hare had just walked past an army check point on the way to church when moments later she lay dying on a country road, shot in the back by a paratrooper.[11] They are campaigning for justice in relation to a number of other incidents of unarmed people shot and left to die on the roadside by British soldiers, like Fergal Caraher, shot dead by soldiers in front of witnesses as he drove home on a South Armagh road.[12]

In the village of Aughnacloy, County Tyrone, 24-year old Aidan McAnespie was shot in the back while walking through a border check point on his way to a Gaelic football match.[13] British soldiers made clear their hostility and warned him on several occasions that they were going to 'get him', his brother Vincent recalled. They did get him on 21 February 1988.The anguish of the family was compounded by the fact that no soldier has ever been held to account for Aidan's death. In recent years when instructed to observe a minute's silence by football authorities on remembrance weekend a section of the Celtic support have refused to be silent and instead sung the ballad of Aidan McAnespie in tribute to the young Tyrone man whose life was ended by a British bullet. In June 2018 the former Grenadier Guardsman David Holden was charged with manslaughter and gross negligence in connection with McAnespie's death, having been charged once already in 1990 though then the case was dropped.[14]

Contrary to the British media narrative British soldiers were never considered peace keepers by the nationalist population but rather oppressors. Any nationalist opposition to the British presence was ruthlessly dealt with by the state. The response was emergency laws, internment without trial, harassment, torture and intimidation. British policy has been responsible for the deaths of children, women and youths caused by rubber and plastic bullets and widespread collusion between British security forces and loyalist paramilitary gangs targeting nationalists for summary execution. Punishment beatings and degrading strip searches of male and female prisoners was the norm. Soldiers with the full knowledge of their government engaged in a litany of human rights abuses on a systematic basis. Awareness of such actions may help readers outside Ireland understand why the remembrance poppy is viewed in less than glowing terms in Ireland.

To display the red poppy has been a signifier of British identity and support for the British Army presence in Ireland. This is why it is such a divisive symbol. Many unionists wear it as a sign of their Britishness. Many nationalists reject the poppy because of its link to British militarism and identity. Irrespective of the peace process to this day the poppy is irrevocably mired in the divisive politics of Northern Ireland and remains a polarising and contested symbol. Far from being neutral or benign it is political and partisan. That is why footballer James McClean has said he would not wear a poppy on his football jersey while playing for West Bromwich Albion – and likewise Wigan and Sunderland football teams. He has suffered media criticism, abuse online and at football grounds across England for his stance. But the young footballer from Derry did not shy away from his refusal to wear the red poppy. In the West Brom match day programme he explained that he 'would wear it every day of the year' if it only represented those who died in the two world wars. But, he pointed out, the poppy commemorated the British military killed in all conflicts the UK had been involved in, including the north of Ireland. He could never under any circumstances have anything to do with it in that:

> Because of the history where I come from in Derry. I cannot wear something that represents that.[15]

In 1972, in Derry, 14 unarmed civilians were murdered in cold blood by the parachute regiment while taking part in a demonstration against internment without trial. In the years that followed British soldiers would go on to kill many more unarmed nationalist residents of Derry. It was the killings on what became known as Bloody Sunday, though, that left the deepest scar, and a burning hatred for the parachute regiment in particular. The nationalist community perception was not just that British soldiers murdered unarmed people but that they were able to do so with impunity. This is why James McClean, like other nationalists, rejects the poppy.

In a gerrymandered state dominated by a unionist hegemony from its creation in 1921, nationalists were continually reminded of their inferior position. Discrimination against Catholics in jobs, housing and the lack of political power was institutionalised – a situation successive British governments did everything to support.[16] Remembrance Day events along with other activities on the Orange Order calendar were expressions of British identity. The poppy became part of the cultural paraphernalia of unionist domination. Unionist hegemony in effect meant that to not wear a poppy in certain work places meant not to have a job. The wearing of a poppy was obligatory in many work and public places. Right up to this day not wearing a poppy in certain places can mean being stopped and beaten.[17]

The politics of suspicion and hostility surrounding the poppy have not disappeared since the peace process. Disputes about the emblem continue in the work place and in other areas of life. It has also provoked unease within public broadcasting. Complaints emerged of undue pressure placed on presenters to wear the emblem. In 2015 a whistle-blower came forward to report that BBC Northern Ireland presenters had no choice but to wear the poppy on air and are effectively forced into the decision. A BBC insider revealed that, 'if a decision by a studio-based presenter not to wear a poppy were to arise they'd be asked to take annual leave'. While BBC bosses insist wearing the poppy on screen is a personal choice, when asked if presenters who refused to wear a poppy would be reassigned to off-screen duties, a BBC spokesman refused to deny it. Clara Reilly, the chair of 'Relatives for Justice', which represents relatives of those killed by British soldiers, insisted that journalists in the north should not be compelled to wear the symbol. Reilly, who was contacted by the whistle-blower, appealed to the BBC to 'consider the views of the whole community, claiming the corporation was failing as a neutral and acceptable public broadcasting service'. Mary Kate Quinn, whose uncle, John Laverty, was one of ten innocent Catholics killed by the parachute regiment in Ballymurphy in West Belfast in August 1971, asked: 'Will the BBC issue a clear statement saying that the wearing of a poppy does not commemorate the RUC, UDR and the British army as part of Operation Banner and the conflict in the north?' The BBC declined to comment.[18] The symbolism is clear: the poppy commemorates British forces who fought in every conflict. That includes Operation Banner, the name for the occupation of the six counties by British troops.

Northern Ireland under British occupation

Students at Queen's University Belfast have protested over sales of British Legion poppies on the premises with one motion to the Students' Union saying that: 'the poppy appeal is a politically charged and necessarily divisive initiative, given the nature of local politics'.[19] In March 2018 Derry and Strabane Council voted to stop British armed forces from recruiting or advertising in schools. Independent councillor Gerry Donnelly put forward the motion calling on schools 'to refuse British armed forces access to children/pupils as part of their attempt to glamourise/recruit for their imperialist ventures'. Donnelly has long argued that people who support such bans on British soldiers from local schools and other venues see symbols like the poppy as stained with the blood of innocent people, and that the British troops are not peacekeepers but oppressors.

Most people who make a donation and pin on a poppy do so for honourable reasons. However, the record of the British Army in Ireland is far from honourable. Across the six counties dozens of campaigns and independent enquiries are under way bringing to light the full scale of army atrocities. Successive British governments tried hard to bury these deeds from public and media gaze but they have failed. These campaigns for justice and truth are largely made up of the relatives of those killed. For example, the 'Ballymurphy Massacre Campaign' is fighting to highlight the murder over a 3-day period of 11 unarmed civilians including a Catholic priest by the parachute regiment. These killings occurred between 9 and 11 August 1971, in the Ballymurphy housing estate in West Belfast.[20]

There were numerous other killings of unarmed civilians in the Ballymurphy area alone over the years. But like the many hundreds of other cases across the north, in almost every instance no soldier was ever held to account for these killings. A rare exception was the murder of Thomas 'Kidso' Reilly. Private Ian Thain shot Kidso in the back and was convicted of murder in 1984. Two years later Thain was released on licence and was back serving with his British Army regiment. Kidso, 22, was home in Belfast for a short holiday. He had been a road manager with a number of 1980s pop groups in England. Thousands attended his funeral, including members of the female band Bananarama, for whom he had worked. There were also flowers and cards from Paul Weller and the group Spandau Ballet who knew him. Speaking after the end of the conflict in 2007, when the British soldiers had left the north, Kidso's brother Michael said:

When you've had experience of the British Army in the way my family have you can honestly say nothing good ever came out of them being here…You'd like to think lessons have been learned but now we see the same thing happening all over again in Iraq, you wonder how many more innocent victims like my brother have been created there.[21]

Kidso Reilly was an avid Celtic supporter and travelled to Glasgow to see the team often. On the anniversary of his death family and friends displayed a banner in tribute to the young man at Celtic Park. Years later supporters would unfurl a huge anti-war banner in opposition to the poppy at Celtic stadium which read: 'No blood-stained poppy on our Hoops'. A banner which provoked much controversy, debate and a witch hunt against those people who unfurled the anti-poppy statement.

For many Protestants and unionists, the poppy is a symbol of respect for the war dead and also a potent symbol of their Britishness. By contrast for many Catholics and republicans it stands for Empire, oppression and the British occupation. Protestants volunteered in large numbers to fight in the First World War and were largely gathered in the 36th Ulster Division. At the Battle of the Somme in 1916 the 36th suffered catastrophic losses when they went over the top. Many members of the Ulster Volunteer Force (UVF) formed a couple of years earlier to oppose Irish Home Rule had joined the 36th Division. Ever since, unionists commemorate those men who lost their lives on the Somme. However, with the onset of the Troubles in 1969-70 a new paramilitary loyalist group emerged called the Ulster Volunteer Force (UVF). Ostensibly it was formed to fight to maintain the six counties as part of Britain and resist a united Ireland. In reality, it was made up of sectarian murder gangs who terrorised and murdered Catholics. It drove thousands of Catholics from their homes and jobs. It murdered many hundreds of people often with the active collusion of British military intelligence. Today in some loyalist housing estates there are giant wall murals painted on the gable-end walls to commemorate the UVF who fought on the Somme but also to commemorate more recent UVF members who murdered Catholics. In some of these paintings, masked gun men pose in emulation of the guard of honour that attends Armistice Day commemorations, adorned with red poppies. The message from these murals is clear. They draw a visceral connection between the UVF in the Somme and the UVF of more modern times who murdered Catholics and are celebrated as heroes. Such murals leave little room for ambiguity. In this context the poppy is dripping red with the blood of innocent Catholics. The poppy may be cherished by many unionists but such wall murals featuring the poppy and loyalist murder gangs only reinforce nationalist hostility to this image of remembrance. The elision of the commemoration of the British dead and loyalist murder gangs are not isolated incidents: they are common. In South Belfast less than a mile from the Ormeau Road betting shop where five Catholics were gunned down and killed in a notorious sectarian killing by a Ulster Defence Association (UDA) murder squad, a plaque adorned with remembrance poppies commemorates these UDA killers alongside another plaque commemorating the British soldiers killed in the Great War.[22] In the lower Shankill area of Belfast a wall mural emerged in 2014 honouring a UDA gunman replete with poppy and First World War imagery headed with the words 'Remember With Pride'. Here the poppy is invoked to remember both slaughter on the Somme and those who slaughtered Catholics. In Moygashel, near Dungannon in county Tyrone, a commemorative banner was erected to Wesley Sommerville in 2014. He was a soldier in the British Army Ulster Defence Regiment and also a UVF loyalist paramilitary. He was involved in the murder of Catholics and died alongside three members of the Miami Showband whom he set out to murder when his UVF bomb exploded prematurely.[23] The tribute to Sommerville as a loyalist paramilitary and British soldier helps explain why many nationalists view British soldiers and loyalist collusion as systemic and why they find the poppy which commemorates such people so hard to stomach.

A mural to Trevor King, UVF killer and British agent

When families of nationalists killed by British soldiers have called
for those responsible to be held to the same standards of justice
as other parties to the conflict and stand trial, British politicians
and media have screamed outrage. The *Daily Telegraph, Times*
and *Daily Mail* have all published editorials expressing anger
at the 'unfair treatment' of British soldiers under scrutiny by
the Historical Investigations Unit (heir to the Police Service's
Historical Enquiries Unit). Prime Minister Theresa May stood up
in the House of Commons in May 2018 to complain that British
Army veterans were being 'unfairly targeted for investigation'
in relation to legacy killings in Northern Ireland. This claim was
repeated mantra like by Conservative and Labour politicians.
The claims were entirely incorrect. Figures produced by the
Police Service of Northern Ireland reveal that it is not British
Army but IRA killings that constitute the majority of cases due
to be investigated.[24] This has not stopped headlines in the British
Press like 'Betrayal of our Soldiers Again' and 'Veterans hit out
at "treachery" of ministers over IRA killings probe'. A series
of high profile generals lined up to protest at the prospect of

British soldiers being held to account for killing nationalists. Lord Dannatt, head of the Army between 2006 and 2009, expressed disgust at the prospect of prosecuting soldiers for killing Catholics. He told the *Sunday Express*: 'War is hell. War is chaotic. And the IRA was at war with the UK.'

Colonel Richard Kemp, who saw active duty in Bosnia, Iraq and Afghanistan as well as Northern Ireland, said he was, 'so outraged I am returning the prized commission given to me by the Queen'.[25] There is a good argument to be made for a general amnesty from prosecution for all actions committed as part of the conflict. There is a case, too, that it ought to be the commanding officers and the political leaders, not the ordinary soldiers, who should carry the blame for what happened. But what the British generals, politicians and media are arguing for is an end to investigations into British Army killings. The message this sends out is one of double standards and that those killed by British soldiers are less important than other victims. Such presumptions only add to the hostility with which nationalists in the north of Ireland view British militarism and the poppy.

After the First World War it was seen as an embarrassment or a source of shame by many in the new independent Irish Free State to admit that you fought or had relatives who fought for the British. For many relatives it was not something that they wanted publicly to acknowledge in the new Irish Republic that had fought a war to win its freedom from Britain. In recent years the mood has changed. There is a desire to know more about Irish men who died in 1914-18. Starting with the 'peace process' and the Good Friday Agreement of 1998, but particularly since the centenary of the First World War in 2014, there have been a series of initiatives to rehabilitate the poppy and politics of remembrance across Ireland. These actions to improve the image of the poppy are aimed in particular at non-unionists in the south of Ireland. Almost 50,000 Irish men, drawn from every one of the 32 counties in Ireland, lost their lives in the Great War. Some now argue that the poppy is a legitimate way of commemorating Irish relatives who served in the First World War.[26]

Another side of the renewed focus on the Great War is also a desire to promote reconciliation in the context of a peace process between nationalists and unionists. Thus, the centenaries of the start of the First World War, and of the 1916 Rising have been collapsed together in what is now referred to as the 'decade of centenaries' and packaged as a means of promoting respect and mutual understanding between the two sides when it comes to remembering those who fought for Britain in the Great War and those who rose up against British rule in the Easter Rising. Many politicians and academics now talk about a 'shared history' in Ireland, suggesting a kind of commemorative trade-off, whereby nationalists celebrate the Easter Rising, unionists celebrate the Somme and both sides congratulate each other on their tolerance and maturity.

In the Republic of Ireland, the role of Irish men who fought for Britain is increasingly discussed and remembered in an uncritical way. President Higgins and Taoiseach Leo Varadkar now regularly attend British Legion and British Government events to commemorate the First World War. Taoiseach Varadkar has taken to wearing a new emblem, which is the poppy adorned with a shamrock with the motto 'Lest We Forget' across the bottom. The 'Shamrock Poppy' sold in Ireland by the Royal British Legion is designed specifically to recognise Irish soldiers who fought in the First World War declared Varadkar.[27] Unfortunately for the British Legion and Leo Varadkar the Shamrock Poppy they now promote seems to have been inspired by a shamrock and red hand of Ulster design used by the Young Citizen Volunteers who are the youth wing of the UVF. This is the same pro-British organisation responsible for the murder of over 550 men, women and children in the north.[28]

Attempts to make a moral distinction between those Irish men who fought for the British Army in the First World War and those

Irish Republicans who fought against the British Empire and for independence in the Easter Rising are now discouraged.[29] The Easter Rising had two aims – to win Irish independence from the British Empire and to bring an end to the imperialist blood-letting of the First World War. But now, in a misguided wish to bolster the peace process in the north of Ireland, people are asked to suspend critical judgement on the rights and wrongs of that period. But to do so is to lose oneself in non- judgementalism and relativism. It means making no distinction between those who fought and slaughtered for colonialism in the Great War and those who fought for Irish freedom and opposed the slaughter of 1914-18. We should not be prepared to massage the history and politics of 1916 on the Somme or at the GPO to feel good about the present. To do so contrives an ahistorical and retrospective ideal about the legacy of 1916 and other events in order to bolster the contemporary peace process. Those republicans who fought for Irish freedom and self-determination in the Easter Rising were engaged in a progressive and anti-imperialist cause aimed at ending the horror of the First World War. Those Irishmen who fought for the British Empire in the killing fields of Flanders were, by contrast, serving imperialism. Tragically these men fought for the wrong country and died for the wrong cause.

It is an important thing to investigate the First World War, as it is to remember the dead of that war. It is a proper human desire for people to know more about their relatives and forebears' involvement and experience of 1914-18. Indeed, both authors of this book had relatives who joined the British Army. It is entirely possible for the conflict to be researched and discussed without it being a contribution to the glorification of senseless slaughter. A good example is the series of thoughtful debates and exhibitions in the heart of republican West Belfast put on by historians and relatives of men who went to the trenches of the Great War with the Connaught Rangers regiment of the British Army. The work of Belfast historian Philip Orr is another case in point. His work documenting the personal stories of working-class men from Protestant backgrounds who joined the 36th Division is a fine example of broadening our understanding of the central importance of the Somme in the unionist psyche. However, we have seen commemoration being replaced by a kind of unquestioning nostalgia about Irish participation in the slaughter of the First World War.[30]

Nostalgia of this kind is partly due to the influence of the British establishment trying to re-cast the war as a defence of democracy against Prussian militarism – while conveniently forgetting the nature of the other allied powers, such as the brutal colonial record of the Belgians, Tsarist tyranny and, most of all, forgetting Britain's own colonial and authoritarian record.

Those who promote the fuzzy nostalgia encouraged by Poppy Day in the Republic of Ireland are retrospectively justifying the slaughter of 1914-18.[31] They engage in a deceit when they claim that those who fought for Britain were airbrushed out of history in the new Irish state and that the Shamrock Poppy is about rehabilitating such men and giving them their rightful place in history and remembrance. This is very far from the truth. In the newly established Irish Republic, Remembrance Day commemorations did take place in Dublin and other cities to remember the war dead of 1914-18. Wisely, the greater part of Irish society remembered the war as a tragic waste of life.

The veterans of the First World War were not air brushed out of history. Rather, most Irish people judged taking part in a colonial war a mistake and something Irish people should have avoided. As historian Brian Hanley correctly points out, the new Irish Free State that emerged after 1921 emerged because of a rejection of the British Empire, inspired to a great degree by revulsion at the 1914-18 war.[32]

Overwhelmingly the experience of British armed forces in Ireland has been a negative one. Murders, summary executions and burnings of towns like Cork and Balbriggan by the British auxiliaries, the 'Black and Tans', in the Irish war of independence are the legacy. So brutal were the Black and Tans that the Catholic cardinal of Ireland referred to them as a 'horde of savages, some of them simply brigands, burglars and thieves'.

In one of the many hundreds of human rights abuses recorded the late Lord Longford wrote of the 'Tans' torturing captured republicans, 'cutting out the tongue of one, the nose of another, the heart of another and battering in the skull of a fourth'. Their own commander, General Frank Crozier, resigned in 1921 because they had been 'used to murder, rob, loot and burn up the innocent because they could not catch the few guilty on the run'.[33] In what became known as Bloody Sunday, the Black and Tans fired on a crowd attending a Gaelic football match at Croke Park killing 11 and wounding at least 60 others – three of whom later died from their injuries.

No doubt there were many sincere and principled people who wore a British military uniform in Ireland and no doubt the vast majority of people who wear a poppy do so for well-intentioned reasons. But when it comes to Ireland the poppy is a fiercely contested symbol. It provokes support and scorn in equal measure. The hostility is borne out of the lived experience of many Irish people, past and present. From Bloody Sunday, Dublin 1920 to Bloody Sunday, Derry 1972, the red poppy is seen as a blood-stained symbol. It does not conjure up images of bravery, self-sacrifice or the fight for democracy as Theresa May recently claimed.[34] Rather it represents the denial of democracy and freedom and the ending of innocent lives.

Chapter Six

A Century of British Militarism

It was the 'war to end all wars' – but what was Britain's record of keeping the peace since 11 November 1918?

When the war against the Central Powers was over, the British Army launched a number of military operations across the world.

Who were the targets of those actions?

First and foremost it was those countries who had been allies of Britain during the war of 1914-18 that were subject to military intervention in the years that followed. In the period 1919-23 the British Army waged war against the following countries: Russia, in the 'War of Intervention'; India, in a series of policing operations; Ireland, the former British colony that declared its independence in 1916, and reaffirmed it in 1919; Iraq, the Arab nation that had sided with Britain and the Entente to fight against the Ottoman Empire in the 'Arab Revolt'; and Egypt, Britain's 'veiled protectorate'. A report in the *The Worker* for 6 September 1919 pointed out that 'at the time of writing the British troops on the various war fronts amount to over 300,000.' They broke that down as follows:

North Russia 20,000 or more, Siberia 1400, Black Sea and Caucasus 44,000, Egypt and Palestine 96,000, Mesopotamia 21,000, India, 62,000, Ireland 60,000, besides at least 100,000 guarding German prisoners in France.

Each one of these allies and former allies was subject to the most punitive attacks, immediately after the Great War was concluded. In each case the demands of fighting a war alongside Britain, or under British command, had raised expectations of just rewards only for them to be dashed, provoking such a reaction that the Court of St James felt it necessary to crush those rebellious former allies. The wars and policing operations that Britain fought in the immediate aftermath of the Great War visited terrible hardship on those very peoples who had been rallied to support the Entente in their fight against the Central Powers.

British intervention in Russia

British general F. C. Poole landed at Archangel on 1 August 1918. Britain's excuse was that since the Russians had left the war under the Treaty of Brest-Litovsk that March, up to 70 German divisions were free to be moved to the Western Front. Quickly it became clear that the British were not there to fight the Germans at all, but to fight the Russians. Straight away Major-General Poole 'believed that he could effectively act on initiative with impunity' and saw himself from the start 'as a viceroy ruling over a dependant people'. Poole saw the North Russian Government under the Social Revolutionary Nicholas Chaikovsky as 'a purely administrative authority and preferred to deal with Commander Chaplin of the pre-revolutionary Russian Navy and his followers'. With Poole's connivance, Chaplin overthrew Chaikovsky's civilian administration, and Poole's forces pushed 300 miles south of Murmansk. The Bolsheviks halted the allied advance around 150 miles inland on the river Dwina by the railway link to Volodga. On 10 August, the War Office told Poole to 'take the field side by side with the [White Russian] Allies for the recovery of their country'.

The war was undeclared and savage. Corporal V. F. King remembered:

When you got into a village you had to clear the village out as soon as you ever came across any men. They weren't Bolsheviks. They were loyal Russians they used to tell you

113

but as soon as your back was turned they were Bolsheviks again.[1]

'We used gas shells on the Bolsheviki,' Ralph Albertson, a YMCA official who was in North Russia in 1919, wrote in his book, *Fighting Without a War:*

> We fixed all the booby traps we could think of when we evacuated villages. Once we shot more than thirty prisoners... And when we caught the Commissar of Borok, a sergeant tells me he left his body in the street, stripped, with sixteen bayonet wounds. We surprised Borok, and the Commissar, a civilian, did not have time to arm himself...I have heard an officer tell his men repeatedly to take no prisoners, to kill them even if they came in unarmed...I saw a disarmed Bolshevik prisoner, who was making no trouble of any kind, shot down in cold blood...Night after night the firing squad took out its batches of victims.

General Poole had to explain himself in a leaflet: 'We are not fighting Russia or honest Russians,' he wrote. 'We are fighting Bolsheviks, who are the worst form of criminals.'[2]

By the early part of 1919 the British forces in Archangel and Murmansk numbered 18,400. Fighting side by side with them were 5100 Americans, 1800 Frenchmen, 1200 Italians, 1000 Serbs and approximately 20,000 White Russians.[3]

Lieut.-Colonel Sherwood-Kelly, VC, back in England from commanding a battalion of the Hampshire Regiment in North Russia, wrote to a newspaper that:

> the troops of the Relief Force which we were told had been sent out purely for defensive purposes were being used for offensive purposes on a large scale, and far in the interior, in furtherance of some ambitious plan of campaign, the nature

of which we were not allowed to know...

Worse, 'the much-vaunted "loyal Russian Army", composed largely of Bolshevik prisoners dressed in khaki, was utterly unreliable, always disposed to mutiny, and...constituted a greater danger to our troops than the Bolshevik armies opposed to them'. Sherwood-Kelly concluded, perceptively, that 'the puppet Government set up by us in Archangel rested on no basis of public confidence and support and would fall to pieces the moment the protection of British bayonets was withdrawn'.[4]

In the east the anti-Bolshevik General Kolchak at Omsk in the Urals was being supplied by Britain on the advice of British General Alfred Knox: 'Between October 1918 and October 1919, Britain sent to Omsk 97,000 tons of supplies, including 600,000 rifles, 6,831, machine guns, and over 200,000 uniforms.' He also had two British Army battalions.[5]

Britain also supplied General Denikin's forces in the south sending:

full British army kit for half a million men, 1,200 field guns with almost two million rounds of ammunition, 6,100 machine guns, 200,000 rifles with 500 million rounds of ammunition, 629 lorries and motorcars, 279 motorcycles, 74 tanks, six armoured cars, 200 aircraft, twelve 500-bed hospitals, 25 field hospitals and a vast amount of signal and engineer equipment.[6]

The post-war government in Britain was fearful that the public would find out that they were fighting a war against Bolshevik Russia and kept up the charade that they were only providing support. Still, 'the officers of the Royal Tank Corps started to act as tactical commanders of Denikin's armoured corps also to take part in fighting as vehicle commanders and crewmembers'. Major

Bruce's tank detachment's role in taking Tsaritsyn was used as a model in British military training. Similarly, the British Cabinet was told that the Royal Air Force support to Denikin was in a training role, though in fact the 47th Squadron, a combat division, was sent, and in the battle of Tsaritsyn – 'British planes bombed and strafed the Red positions and lines of communication on a daily basis'. Under public pressure over its undeclared war in Russia, the Cabinet announced that the 47th Squadron was disbanded – though in fact just the name was changed and the bombardments carried on.[7]

Despite the British, French and American allies' attempt to distance themselves from direct responsibility for the 'White Army' and their campaign, it became clear that without western support Denikin, Kolchak and the rest had no real appeal to the mass of Russian people. Rich in British arms, their troops melted away. The barbarism of the White Armies, though, was legendary. A letter written by one White Army executioner on the Don gives a flavour of their approach:

> The harvest was pretty good and every evening, apart from the tribunal, numerous Bolshevik prisoners were disposed of – sometimes a hundred, sometimes three hundred, and in one night 500 were dispatched. The mode of procedure was as follows: fifty men dug their own common grave, then they were shot and the other fifty men would cover them up and dig a new grave, side by side, and so on. There are so many of them that we have decided to their great discomfiture to turn Red Guards into slaves.[8]

Red Army commander Leon Trotsky protested:

> the women and children of Archangel and Astrakhan are maimed and killed by English airmen with the aid of English Explosives. English ships bomb our shores...

Churchill's undeclared war against Russia was deeply unpopular in Britain. The Press called it Mr Churchill's Private War. A 'Hands Off Russia' campaign was very successful. One of its organisers, William Paul, wrote that 'If labour in this country can exert itself to protest effectively in every field of activity, then it may compel the British Government to abandon its armed expedition in Russia.' London dock workers refused to coal the SS Jolly George, a munitions ship on its way to Russia. Rail workers also tried to disrupt the munitions going to the intervention forces.[9]

1919-21: The War of Independence in Ireland

More than 200,000 Irishmen fought for Britain in the Great War, and around 40,000 lost their lives. But from 1916 to 1922 Britain fought a war against a risen Irish people, determined to be free. In 1916 the British forces put down the Easter Rebellion executing its leaders. But the country was still in open defiance. Mass meetings outside churches committed the faithful to refuse

The Auxiliary 'Black and Tans' wreaked havoc in Ireland

conscription and in much of the country the Irish Republican Army was the acknowledged law. The United Kingdom's General Election of November 1918 saw Sinn Fein candidates elected in 73 of the 101 constituencies in Ireland. The Sinn Fein MPs would not sit in Westminster, but declared themselves representatives of an Irish Parliament, the Daíl.

From among its demobbed soldiers Britain recruited an 'Auxiliary' force of 14,000 to back up the Royal Irish Constabulary, known, because of their mix of black police and khaki military uniforms, as the 'Black and Tans'.

The auxiliaries and the RIC imposed 'a state of government terrorism' according to the *New Statesman*. In September 1920 they sacked Balbriggan, terrorising the citizens of that town, murdering two Irish nationalists, beating many others and burning many shops and houses. On 21 November – Bloody Sunday – the auxiliaries and the Royal Irish Constabulary opened fire on the crowd at a Gaelic football match at Croke Park. Fourteen were killed and at least 60 wounded.[10]

India: 1919

The contribution of the British-Indian Army to the war was profound. With an army of more than a million men India's army was as many again as those who fought in the British Army. Indian troops fought courageously at Ypres, Neuve Chapelle and Gallipoli. In the Middle East and North Africa, Indian troops shouldered the lion's share of British efforts. At the end of the war they had a real expectation that they would be rewarded with self-government, comparable to that enjoyed by Canada, Australia and New Zealand. But they were betrayed. The 'Montagu-Chelmsford Reforms' of 1918 offered no substantial role to Indians in their own government beyond the lowest local questions (less than half of the legislative council members were to be elected, and power retained by the governor). British MP Vickerman Rutherford declared that:

Never in the history of the world was such a hoax perpetrated on a great people as England perpetrated upon India, when in return for India's invaluable service during the War, we gave to the Indian nation such a discreditable, disgraceful, undemocratic, tyrannical constitution.

Denying any meaningful self-government, the British administration went one step further, when the puppet legislative council passed the 'Anarchical and Revolutionary Crimes Act of 1919', known as the 'Rowlatt Act' after the judge Sir Sidney Rowlatt, whose committee drew up its provisions. Under the Rowlatt Act, suspects could be detained indefinitely, tried in camera and allegations made anonymously – all adding up to a fearsome set of measures to silence and intimidate Indian nationalists.

In March and April of 1919 a number of stoppages – hartals – were made to protest against the Rowlatt Act. On 9 April the government responded by jailing two nationalist leaders

Despite sending more than a million soldiers to fight for Britain in the Great War, Indians were refused self-government afterwards

in the Punjab: Dr Saifuddin Kithclew and Dr Satyapal. There were riots in the town of Amritsar. The police opened fire on the crowd killing ten, and in the rioting that followed five Englishmen were killed. The town was shut down by Brigadier General Reginald Dyer. On the 13 April a religious festival, Baisakhi, drew crowds of 10,000 or more, who were gathered in the walled gardens called Jallianwala Bagh. Dyer ordered his men to surround the garden and open fire on the crowd, until their ammunition was spent. Three hundred and twenty-nine people were killed outright and 1179 were wounded after 1650 rounds were fired.

Shocking as it was, the Jallianwala Bagh massacre was only the culmination of Dyer's reign of terror. He arrested students and teachers and made them crawl on their bellies in the street. He had hundreds of people flogged and built an open cage in the town centre to detain people. He had Sadhus painted with quick lime and left to dry in the sun. And he had aircraft bomb villagers as they worked in the fields.[11]

Iraq: 1920

An uprising of Arabs and Kurds against the imposition of the Sykes-Picot division of Arabia came quickly after the end of the war. In May of 1920 they rose against the 100,000 British and Indian troops that were holding the territory.

The Royal Air Force:

flew missions totalling 4,008 hours, dropped 97 tons of bombs and fired 183,861 rounds for the loss of nine men killed, seven wounded and 11 aircraft destroyed behind rebel lines. The rebellion was thwarted, with nearly 9,000 Iraqis killed.[12]

The Air Minister, Lord Thomson, wrote about one district of 'recalcitrant chiefs' in the Liwa region on the Euphrates in November 1923: 'As they refused to come in, bombing was then authorised and took place over a period of 2 days. The surrender of many of the headmen of the offending tribes followed.'[13]

The bombardment of Iraq was a big step for the Royal Air Force. The government congratulated them on achieving air superiority to hold land that even thousands of troops could not. The RAF felt they had learned that aerial bombardment could cow populations. British military leaders broke the taboo against aerial bombardment in Iraq. One of the squadron leaders there was Arthur Harris who, in 1942, would organise the campaign to destroy Dresden and other German cities by air power.

In 1939 Britain and Germany were once again at war, and once again the war became a world war. (We have written about this before in the 2011 book *Unpatriotic History of the Second World War*). In total 60 million lost their lives. Today we look at the Second World War as a struggle between democracy and Fascism. But at the time much of what the British Army did was to fight over who controls the colonies. Between 1940 and 1944 the contest between Germany and Britain was fought over possession of North Africa – without any thought for the people who lived there. Elsewhere, too, the British Army fought for the possession of strategic territories.

Iran: 1941

In 1941 Britain invaded Iran, deposing Reza Shah and putting his 21-year old son Reza Pahlavi on the throne. The British-Indian Army occupied the oilfields at Mosul. The action was coordinated with the Soviet Union, which invaded the north of the country as the British-Indian Army invaded the south. Maintaining order in occupied Iran proved a disaster for the Iranians. Making it the supply hub between the Soviet Union and British India skewed the economy dangerously. The allied forces buying power contrasted with the low wages of Iranians led to a spiral of inflation that pushed bread out of most people's price range. Hunger led to rioting. On 8 December 1942 British troops fired on protesting students, killing scores and wounding hundreds.

India: 1942

On 7 August 1942, frustrated at the decades of British opposition to self-rule, the All-India Congress Committee meeting in Bombay passed a resolution demanding that Britain 'Quit India'. Within 36 hours the entire leadership of the Congress Party was jailed. In the first wave 60,222 protestors were arrested and 18,000 jailed under the Defence of India Rules. The total eventually jailed rose as high as 90,000.

Britain's suppression of the Quit India movement drew British troops away from the conflict with Germany, and troops fired on Indian protestors. At the time the numbers killed were acknowledged to be hundreds but estimates today put the total at around ten thousand. To impose order, the British brought in a 'whipping act'.

With the Congress leaders in jail, India was dangerously unstable. Britain was holding the country by force, but still dependent upon India's tax base and its soldiers to fight the Second World War. Bengal's grain was being used to feed the Ceylon rubber workers. Churchill had been warned that the state was dangerously undersupplied, but the War Cabinet ignored the prospect of famine. They were not just indifferent, but hostile to Bengalis, many of whom were sympathetic to the Indian National Army, which was working alongside the Japanese to overthrow British rule. As the Japanese forces advanced towards Bengal, the British authorities set about making sure that the province was inhospitable, wrecking boats, bicycles and even cooking pots as the remaining grain stores were relocated out. The famine was drastic. Eventually as many as 3.5 million died. Subhas Chandra Bose, leader of the Indian National Army, offered aid to Bengal from the grain surplus in Burma, but fearing a propaganda coup, the British administration refused the offer.

'Dekemvriana': 1944

ELAS resistance fighters liberated much of the inland of Greece taking on the Italian and German occupation forces between 1940 and 1944. They were on paper British allies. But in 1942, the exiled Greek Army in Egypt had rebelled against their Royalist officers in favour of the new partisan leadership. The British responded by turning their guns on the Greeks and putting them in camps without water or food to break their will. Churchill knew how determined the Greek resistance fighters were, but he also had an agreement with Stalin that Greece would be part of Britain's 'sphere of influence' after the war. In 1944 as the German forces were on the retreat, and without telling the Cabinet, Churchill ordered General Scobie 'to act as if you were in a conquered city where a local rebellion was in progress'. 'We have to hold and dominate Athens,' he added.

The 2nd Parachute Brigade and the 5th (Scottish) Parachute Battalion were among those used to suppress the victorious

Britain's allies in Greece, the Security Battalions assassinated the leaders of the wartime resistance to Nazi rule

Greek resistance. In Syntagma Square a parade of national liberation was fired upon leaving scores dead. In Greece these came to be known as the Dekemvriana, the 'December Days'. By the end of December the British forces were 75,000 strong. To defeat the ELAS resistance the British recruited also the same 'Security Battalions' who had been organised by the German occupation. The Security Battalions were known for their violence and barbarism. To show their success rate they handed sacks of the severed heads of Greek ELAS fighters to their British handlers.

Malaya: 1948-58

In the Second World War the Malayan People's Anti-Japanese Army had fought to free the country, with the support of the British. They were led by Chin Peng and drew on Malaya's large ethnic Chinese population. After the war the British backed decolonisation but under a constitution that disenfranchised the Chinese. To enforce the new constitution Britain sent troops to suppress dissent. Mostly the dissenters were ethnic Chinese, rubber and tin workers and squatters in the forests, but the British branded them 'Communist Terrorists' and set about a brutal campaign against them. The same Chin Peng who had been honoured by the British for fighting against the Japanese was now branded 'Enemy Number One'. High Commissioner Gerald Templer developed a policy for isolating rebel bands by establishing 'an outer ring of ambushes to prevent an exodus from the killing ground'. After starving the bands for a month or so, Templer's men embarked on 'the killing stage'.

In 1948 soldiers of the Scots Guards shot dead 24 unarmed Malaysian villagers at the rubber plantation by Batang Kali village, and then covered up the massacre. According to one of the soldiers, the sergeant told them that 'the villagers are going to be shot and we could fall in or [opt] out'.[14] One officer recalled:

we were shooting people. We were killing them...this was raw savage success, it was butchery. It was horror.

An insight into what the British Army was getting up to in Malaya came when the *Daily Worker* published a photograph of a soldier posing with the heads of two Chinese rebels, one in each hand.

As well as direct engagement, the Royal Air Force was called on to carry out aerial bombardment. There were 4500 air strikes in the first 5 years of the 'Malayan insurgency'. One rebel stronghold was bombed in 1956 with 545,000lbs of bombs, at the beginning of May 1957 with 94,000lbs and then on 15 May with another 70,000lbs.

To try to undermine the popular support for the rebels the British used a policy of relocation into village camps, behind barbed wire. Half a million Chinese were relocated, usually into degrading and impoverished conditions – though the Colonial Office called it 'a great piece of colonial development'. As well as the relocation policy, some 34,000 Malays – mostly of Chinese origin – were detained and some 15,000 exiled altogether.

Decolonisation in Malaya proved to involve even greater domination by the British Army. British strategy was to defeat the nationalist movement before withdrawing, so guaranteeing the installation of a supplicant elite, well-tutored in the terror of British fire power and implicated in the suppression. As many have noted since, the determination to dominate the national movement was also inspired by the economic needs of the British Empire, its reliance on earnings from rubber plantations and tin mines in the immediate post-war period. The anti-insurgency campaign had the advantage of silencing labour activism on the plantations and securing Britain's extensive investments in 'independent' Malaya.[15]

1952-6: Mau Mau uprising

Around 100,000 Kenyans had joined the British forces in the Second World War. When they returned home there was no hero's welcome. European settlers kept the best land in the Central Province uplands – known as the White Highlands – for themselves. Kenyans squatting the land the Europeans did not farm were tolerated as long as they worked as farm labourers – but kept on pitiful wages and evicted when they could no longer work. There was a nationalist campaign, the Kenyan African Union, led by Jomo Kenyatta. But many of the Kikuyu squatters despaired at the glacial pace of change.

A secret society, the Mau Mau, was formed among the Kikuyu squatters. It met at night and bound its members together with a secret oath, much like the rural followers of Ned Ludd in early nineteenth century Britain. They burnt white farms and tried to intimidate those who dealt with them badly. The British authorities reacted with fury.

Though Kenyatta had publicly disowned and denounced the Mau Mau rebels, he was tried for supporting them and sentenced

Mau Mau suspects held in a British concentration camp, 1953

to 7 years in jail. Waging war on the Mau Mau itself the British Army killed as many as 10,000 Kikuyu and other African people. Men were tortured and mutilated with ears and fingers cut off, and beaten all over, often on the soles of the feet and around the groin. The British Army kept score cards to list their 'kills' and paid a £5 reward for the first subunit to kill an insurgent. Apart from those killed in the field, the official execution list recorded 1015 hanged between 1952 and 1956, 297 for murder, 559 for unlawful possession of a firearm or for swearing a Mau Mau oath.

The army cleared 80,000 Kikuyu from the 'White Highlands' and put them behind barbed wire in 'Native Land Units'. This ethnic cleansing led to thousands more deaths. In one camp 400 people came down with Typhus and 90 of them died. One camp commandant later admitted that the Kikuyu detainees were subject to 'short rations, overwork, brutality, humiliating and disgusting treatment and floggings – all in violation of the United Nations Universal Declaration of Human Rights'. The British governor asked the Colonial Secretary in London whether forced labour could be formally re-introduced for the Kikuyu, but he was told that this would be too difficult to manage with world opinion. In the event, the Kikuyu in the camps, as well as the Mau Man prisoners, were regularly subject to forced labour and beatings.[16]

1956 Suez

After the Second World War Egypt had been governed by King Farouk, with the help of the British and the Wafd party. In 1952 a coup by the Free Officers Movement, whose *de facto* leader was a young Corporal Gamal Abdel Nasser, promised Parliamentary elections and an end to corruption. In 1956, as President of the Revolutionary Command Council, Nasser nationalised the Suez Canal Company, owned by Britain and France. British Prime Minister Anthony Eden thought that Nasser must be 'got rid of', 'destroyed', 'murdered'.[17] With the support of Israel and France, Britain planned to invade.

In November 1956, after Israel attacked Egypt, British paratroopers landed to seize Port Said and the neighbouring area. Seven hundred and fifty Egyptians were killed in the attack. One of the paratroopers remembered 'several Wogs appeared running down the street in front of us': 'we kept shooting all the time'. The United Nations forced Britain to accept a ceasefire of 6 November, at the prompting of the United States, whose leaders thought the adventure foolish and dangerous.

Cyprus: 1955-9, 1974

In 1955 a guerrilla group called EOKA (National Organisation of Cypriot Fighters) took up arms against the British colonial authorities on the island. Their goal was freedom from British rule, and 'Enosis', union with Greece, and they were led by Georgios Grivas. 'I can imagine no more disastrous policy for Cyprus than to hand it over to a friendly but unstable power. It would have the effect of undermining the eastern bastion of NATO,' said the Colonial Secretary, Oliver Lyttleton:

> Eastern Mediterranean security demands that we maintain sovereign power in Cyprus.

There were around 1250 EOKA fighters arraigned against 30,000 British troops. There were 1144 exchanges recorded between EOKA and the British forces, and EOKA killed 105 soldiers and another 50 policemen. In 1959 EOKA was persuaded to lay down its arms in exchange for an independent government for Cyprus.

The victor in Cyprus' first election – with 70 per cent of the vote – was Archbishop Makarios who had been exiled from the country by the British authorities. He proved a popular leader in Cyprus but was despised in London and Washington where he was called the 'Castro of the Mediterranean'. In collusion with the Conservative military government in Greece, Georgios Grivas took up arms against Makarios destabilising his government. In 1974 with the connivance of the British and Americans, Turkey invaded the northern part of the island setting up a Turkish government there. The conflict led to a coup against Makarios and a brutal division of the island.

The Aden emergency: 1963-7

In 1956, a young man on his National Service bundled on to a great barge of a troop carrier that made its way lazily through the Mediterranean and the Suez Canal (when you could) with 300 other bored, sunburnt, young men on their way to fight Chin Peng's Malaysian guerrillas.

As they approached the Arabian Peninsula, they were gathered for emergency briefings by their officers: a rebellion had broken out in Yemen – then known as the British colony of Aden and its hinterlands – and they were to land at Aden and put it down. Arriving at night, the squaddies were armed with two-foot batons, and told to put some stick about. There was fighting all through the market port, but in time the British Army prevailed and the Yemenis, bloodied and bruised, cleared the streets. Not much later, the troops were back on the barge, on their way to hunt down Chin Peng.

It was only on the boat, piecing together all their stories as they celebrated another victory for British fair play, that the men worked out that there never had been a rebellion in Yemen. The only fighting that the citizens of Aden did was in reply to the battering that they were getting from the squaddies, and that was mostly just stone-throwing here and there. The whole thing had been made up by the British officers so that their troops would be able to get some action in, let off a bit of steam, and arrive in Singapore with a bit of confidence. In Singapore the soldiers chatted with men who had been there longer. It turned out that the 'rebellion in Aden' was an exercise they had all been on.

In 1963, inspired by Gamal Abdel Nasser's revolution in Egypt, there was an uprising in Yemen. British troops were sent in to put it down. In Aden, in 1966, the British officer commanding, Lieutenant Colonel Colin 'Mad Mitch' Mitchell's brutal war against the guerrillas span so far out of control that he was made to resign. The officers had initiated inter-platoon rivalry by awarding Robertson's jam golliwog stickers to units for each killing of an Arab.[18]

British troops in Aden

In the hinterland, the British used air power to break support for the rebels, as Captain R. A. B. Hamilton of No. 8 Squadron explained:

> The Air Staff would work in the closest contact with the political officer. It was my task, equipped with a portable wireless set, to camp as close to the scene of operations as I considered possible, so as to facilitate the surrender of the tribe and to reduce the extent of the operations to a minimum, Two, and one-day warnings were dropped on the

tribe, followed by an hour's warning before the first attack, so that women and children could be taken to a place of safety and every effort was made to inflict losses to property rather than lives.

The concept of 'proscription' bombing meant that once the leaflets had been dropped, all humans and livestock were legitimate targets within the proscribed area.[19]

In 1967, Yemeni soldiers in the British-backed force were in mutiny and attacked the British troops, killing several. Having lost all support among the Yemenis, Britain withdrew and the National Liberation Front declared Yemeni independence.

Ireland, the longest war: 1969-2007

After the partition of Ireland at the end of the war of independence the six northernmost counties were kept part of Britain and ruled by the Ulster elite as 'a protestant state for a protestant people'. Catholics in the six counties were disenfranchised by gerrymandering of constituencies, and the additional votes afforded businesses, so that all power was in the hands of the unionists. Jobs and social services, too, were kept to the 'loyal' Protestant community, leaving many Catholics living in overcrowded slums, with long stretches out of work.

In 1967 the Northern Ireland Civil Rights Association (NICRA) was set up to fight for 'one man one vote'. Its marches were immediately the target of violent attacks by the Royal Ulster Constabulary and the 'B Specials'. The 'B force' of the Ulster Special Constabulary was recruited out of Edward Carson's paramilitary UVF in October 1920. From then it was on hand as a special sectarian squad to attack Irish nationalists.

On 5 October 1968 NICRA marched in Derry. 'Demonstrators were beat down on the streets.' The more radical People's Democracy organised the next march from Belfast to Derry. The Royal Ulster Constabulary marked the student protestors closely until they came to a bridge at the town of Burntollet on 4 January 1969. A crowd of around 300, mostly off-duty B Specials, attacked the march with a truck load of stones brought from a nearby quarry and beat them with batons.

That summer loyalists planned to attack the Catholic 'Bogside' area of Derry under the cover of the annual Apprentice Boys march. The 'B Specials' were deployed to support them. To their surprise the Bogside organised itself as the Citizens Defence Committee, raised barricades across the streets, and fought the B Specials and the Apprentice Boys to a standstill. Tommy McCourt remembered, 'we thought the cops might get in, but they stopped as they came to the barricade': 'That gave everyone the initial boost that we'd stopped them.' The fighting between the Bogsiders and the RUC went on for 3 days, but Derry remained free.[20]

After the battle of the Bogside, British troops were sent in to 'restore order'. The deployment was called Operation Banner, and it lasted from 1969 to 2007: 38 years. At its height the British military presence in Northern Ireland stood at a remarkable 30,000 troops. At first they were welcomed by some among the nationalist population, but the honeymoon did not last. The British Army took its cue from the politicians who were determined that Britain would not surrender authority in Northern Ireland. That meant that the army were quickly put to use enforcing the suppression of the nationalists.

The Ulster Defence Regiment was created in 1969. In Parliament the MP and civil rights leader Bernadette Devlin challenged Defence Minister Roy Hattersley: 'Can the honourable gentleman give me one concrete statement to show that this is not the Ulster Special Constabulary under the guise of the British Army?' Since it was formed a hundred UDR members have been charged with sectarian murder and over a thousand have reported their weapons 'lost' or stolen.

In 1970 the army's overall commander in Northern Ireland,

Ian Freeland, announced that people with petrol bombs would be shot. That summer Bernadette Devlin was arrested and nationalists rioted. The army imposed a curfew on the Falls Road in Belfast. The army killed four people, including a journalist covering the story.

In February 1971 the army carried out raids in nationalist Belfast leading to 3 days of rioting. In retaliation the Provisional Irish Republican Army, which had been set up the year before, shot dead Private Robert Curtis, the first serving soldier to die in the conflict.

That August the army launched Operation Demetrius, raiding the homes of those who were on the police's list as Republican sympathisers. A total of 342 people were arrested on suspicion of being in the IRA, and, in a sinister new step, were interned in a camp in a former RAF base called Long Kesh. The policy of internment without trial was uniquely unpopular – quite apart from the fact that many of those who were picked up were plainly not any part of the IRA.

On 30 January 1972 a massive demonstration against the internment policy began. General Ford, the army's second in command, had already prepared a memo to General Tuzo saying that 'the minimum force necessary to achieve a restoration of law and order is to shoot selected ringleaders among the' people he called the 'Derry Young Hooligans' (not a name they chose for themselves). The argument that the leaders of the Civil Rights protests 'were enemies of the Crown and should be liable to being shot' was made by Lord Hailsham at a Cabinet Committee the previous year. Ford's plan was approved by the Prime Minister, Edward Heath. The general ordered a parachute regiment into Derry to challenge the protest, against advice from the RUC. Under Lt Col Derek Wilford the regiment opened fire killing 13 protestors. Ever after the day was known as 'Bloody Sunday'.

After Bloody Sunday the Irish Republican Army challenged

British rule in the six counties. There were so many volunteers they had to turn them away. The demand for civil rights within a reformed British state had given way to a revived belief that all 32 counties of Ireland could and should be united and free.

In May 1974 a clandestine unit of the Ulster Defence Regiment made up of Billy Hanna, Robert McConnell and Harris Coyle planted four car bombs in the Irish Republic, in Dublin and Monaghan, that killed 33 people and injured another 300.

Lenny Murphy led a gang of sectarian killers, the Shankill Butchers, who were prosecuted for 19 killings, and, according to author Martin Dillon, probably responsible for another 13. Murphy liked to have his victims hang on a rope while he beat and hacked at their bodies 'much in the manner a sculptor would chip away at a piece of wood or a stone'. Among their number was a member of the Ulster Defence Regiment, Edward McIlwaine. They were assisted by John McFarland Fletcher, a sergeant in the UDR.

Britain's dirty war in Northern Ireland terrorised the nationalist population there. But it did not limit support for the Irish Republican Army or opposition to the British presence. Rather, support for republicanism grew stronger. The numbers interned in Long Kesh grew from around 500 to more than a thousand.

In 1976 Northern Ireland minister Merlin Rees attempted to take back the initiative by reclassifying the interned as criminals, not 'Special Category' prisoners. They were made to wear prison uniforms, and 'convicted' by special 'Diplock courts' that sat without a jury. The prisoners protested the change demanding to be recognised as prisoners of war. After being confined to their cells and stopped from 'slopping out', the prisoners started a hunger strike. In May 1981 Bobby Sands, an IRA prisoner, died in Long Kesh after 66 days without food – to be followed by nine more hunger strikers. Shortly before Sands died he had been elected *in absentia* to the Parliamentary seat of Fermanagh and South Tyrone. More than 100,000 stood to watch his funeral cortege. Support for the political wing of the Republican movement climbed and they won elections in Derry, West Belfast and Fermanagh.

British repression only provoked greater opposition from Northern Ireland's nationalist community

After the upsurge in republican support, British forces began an active policy known as 'shoot-to-kill'. A military group within the Royal Ulster Constabulary called the Headquarters Mobile Support Unit carried out pre-emptive attacks on republicans. In 1982 they shot Michael Tighe and Martin McCauley after waiting for them to return to a weapons dump in a barn. The same year they shot dead Seamus Grew and Roddy Carroll at an RUC checkpoint in Mullacreavie, County Armagh.

Another undercover squad, the Forces Research Unit, ran agents within the loyalist Ulster Defence Association (UDA), including Brian Nelson. Rather than spying on the UDA, they were using Nelson and other loyalists to assassinate republicans. The Forces Research Unit also burnt down the offices of the police chief John Stevens who was called in to investigate the 'shoot-to-kill' policy. In 1989 the human rights lawyer Pat Finucane was shot dead in his home by Ken Barrett. The UDA claimed responsibility for the killing but later they were found to have been helped by the Forces Research Unit.

In June 1991 IRA volunteers Tony Doris, Pete Ryan and Lawrence McNally were ambushed in their car by a Special Air Service shoot-to-kill squad in East Tyrone. Two hundred rounds were fired into their car, which burst into flames. The SAS left the car to burn as a lesson to their families.

In May 1992 the parachute regiment based in Coalisland, County Tyrone rioted attacking local bars. Feargal O'Donnell was savagely beaten across his face. He had eight stitches to close the wound. Attacks like these were commonplace, but this time Feargal's friends fought back. As a crowd gathered to protest the beating, the paratroopers opened fire, wounding three people. Stop and search was a daily event for the young men of the town. 'At Christmas I got tarted up five times and never made Dungannon once,' one man told Fiona Foster. 'I spent two nights in Aughnacloy search centre.'[21]

Britain's war in Northern Ireland wound down when a political compromise was agreed between the Irish Republican Army and the British Government in the 1998 Good Friday Agreement. In exchange for a ceasefire the British guaranteed representation for Irish nationalists within a devolved assembly at Stormont Castle. One thousand and forty-nine from the Crown forces were killed in the fighting, including 705 from the army and 301 from the RUC. Three hundred and thirty-eight Republican fighters were killed, and 1193 civilians.

The Falklands War: 1982

On 2 April 1982, 600 Argentine troops landed at Port Stanley on the Falkland Islands and seized Government House. The islands are 300 miles from Argentina and 8000 miles from Britain. In 1833 Britain seized the Malvinas Islands from Argentina and re-named them. Most of the island is owned by the Falkland Islands Company, created by Royal Charter in 1851. At the time of the invasion the population was 1800.

Britain sent a task force of 100 ships and 26,000 men. Prime Minister Margaret Thatcher explained that it was about prestige: 'Since the Suez fiasco in 1956, British foreign policy had been one long retreat' which she was determined to reverse. Thatcher declared a 200-mile 'exclusion zone' around the islands – extending into Argentina's territorial waters. But when the Argentine cruiser the Belgrano was outside of the exclusion zone, it was fired upon and sunk with the loss of 323 men.

On 21 May 4000 men of the 3rd British Commando landed at San Carlos Bay on the other side of East Falkland, before moving over land to Goose Green and Port Stanley, which they reached on 11 June. After a short battle, the overwhelmed Argentine troops surrendered. There were reports of Argentine prisoners executed after surrendering. One, Corporal Oscar Carrizo, was shot through the head at Mount Longdon after giving up his weapons and jacket. Remarkably, he survived – others were not so lucky:

Also at Mount Longdon, Nestor Flores reports seeing British troops murder privates Quintana, Graminni and Delgado. Corporal Gustavo Osvaldo Pedamonte witnessed the murder of privates Ferreyra, Mosconi, Petruccelli and Maldana by British soldiers. To this must be added the confession of a British former Lance Corporal in 3 Para, who described how he and a colleague had machine-gunned three prisoners they believed to be American mercenaries (who were probably US-educated Argentinians). Ex-Captain Mason says that he told a colonel about the killings at the time. Nothing was done and the colonel has since been promoted to major-general. Similarly, Lucas Morales of Argentina's fifth marine battalion describes being shot at by British troops after surrendering after the battle of Mount William. One British soldier killed during the battle was even found to have a bag full of severed Argentinian ears…

Even after the surrender, Argentine prisoners were executed:

Epifanio Casimiro Benítez testified to further executions of wounded prisoners on 16 July 1982 after the total surrender of Argentinian troops in the Malvinas Islands. Captain Horatio Alberto Bicain claims that he saw British troops kill Captain Artuso after his submarine Sante Fe had been captured.[22]

The war over the Malvinas/Falklands was first and foremost a propaganda exercise. The Falkland islanders' rights were not important to the British Government. Only the year before they had refused an earnest plea from the islanders over the changes in the 1981 Nationality Act that made several hundred of them stateless. Two hundred and fifty-five British servicemen lost their lives in the war. Fifty-six were killed when Argentine aircraft attacked troops landing at Port Pleasant on 8 June 1982. The Royal Navy lost 86 in the Argentine attacks on the ships the Ardent, the Glamorgan, the Sheffield and the Coventry. Six hundred and forty-nine Argentinians were killed – more than half of them in the sinking of the Belgrano. The sacrifice of life, Argentine and British, was all to defend Britain's prestige in the world.

The British Army in the 'New World Order'
In 1991 the Soviet Union was dissolved and the geopolitical contest, the Cold War, that dominated military thinking since 1947 was at an end. US President George H. W. Bush announced a 'New World Order'. Expectations of a 'peace dividend', that swords would be beaten into ploughshares, were disappointed, though. The western powers' victory found them without

an enemy, and so without a *raison d'etre*. Colin Powell, when chairman of the US Joint Chiefs of Staff, said: 'the Soviet Union is gone, the Warsaw Pact is gone, you know, I'm running out of enemies'. In their search for bogeymen to frighten the populace, America went to war against Saddam Hussein and Slobodan Milosevic, but most people could see that these were minor figures, really just whipping boys for the military. As Powell said, ironically, he was 'down to Fidel Castro and Kim Il Sung'. Arbitrary wars were launched, often against former allies from the Cold War era. Their main purpose was not to win wars abroad, but for political leaders to rediscover a sense of purpose at home. Instead of conquering territory and wealth, western leaders pumped themselves up as champions of human rights and ethical intervention.

British soldiers caught up in this new humanitarian imperialism quickly discovered that they were expendable in the struggle for moral authority at home. When military intervention went wrong, soldiers were often blamed for what their generals had commanded them to do. Civil prosecutions of troops for atrocities that were ordered from on high was a further sign of the bad faith of the new humanitarianism.

Bosnia, 1995; Kosovo, 1999

In 1995 the Royal Air Force took part in NATO attacks on the Bosnian Serb forces in the civil war. NATO flew 3515 sorties and a total of 1026 bombs were dropped on 338 Bosnian Serb targets. British forces also took part in the UNPROFOR forces' artillery attacks. In the wake of the peace talks later in 1995 British forces took part in the 'Stabilisation Force' that occupied strategic points in Bosnia. The whole of the Former Yugoslav Republic was placed under a UN 'High Representative' with dictatorial powers to direct and suspend political government. The 'resolution' of the conflict was no such thing, but rather an open invitation to other forces in Yugoslavia to take up arms against their government.

The Kosovo Liberation Army was founded in 1996 to press for the separation of the Yugoslav province. The KLA took up arms against the Federal Republic of Yugoslavia in 1998 and was rewarded with a place at UN sponsored peace talks. When Yugoslav forces took action against Kosovans, NATO launched a prolonged series of air attacks in Kosovo, and against the Yugoslav capital, Belgrade. Rather than calm the conflict the intervention led to more attacks on Kosovans by Yugoslav forces. British Prime Minister Tony Blair tried to persuade US public opinion to support a ground force in Kosovo, earning the jibe that he was willing to fight to the last drop of American blood. Relying on air power, however, the allied forces were only committed to destruction. On 14 April 1999 the allies bombed a convoy of Kosovo Albanian refugees at Korisa – the very people they claimed to be helping – killing 87.

The Royal Air Force played a significant role in the bombardment of Kosovo and of Belgrade. Around 600 people were killed in Kosovo and 5000 in Yugoslavia overall. The citizens of Belgrade protected their bridges from 72 days of aerial bombardment by making themselves 'human shields' – standing on the bridges at night with target signs. Bomb damage to Yugoslavia was estimated at $26 billion. The USAF bombed the Chinese Embassy killing three Chinese reporters. At the time this was claimed to be a result of poor intelligence though it was later shown to be deliberate targeting.[23] In the aftermath of the conflict, 7000 British troops took part in KFOR – a 'stabilisation force'. Under its jurisdiction 20,000 ethnic Serbs were forced out of Kosovo.

Iraq: 1991, 2003

Under Saddam Hussein's dictatorship Iraq invaded Kuwait in 1990. Before then Saddam had been supported by both Washington and London, both because he was a 'strong man' who would face down local radicals, but also later because he was at war with Iran, which since the revolution of 1979 had been a thorn in the side of the western powers. British arms firms' sales to Iraq were supported by the export credits guarantee department – an agency of the Department of Trade and Industry. Thorn EMI, Racal and Marconi Command and Control all made sales to Iraq valued in the millions, underwritten by the ECGD. Saddam Hussein had every reason to expect that the encouragement he got from London and Washington would continue. Broaching the possibility of an invasion of Kuwait, as Iraqi troops massed on the border, US Ambassador April Glaspie assured Saddam that:

> we have no opinion on the Arab-Arab conflicts, like your border disagreement with Kuwait. ...
> James Baker has directed our official spokesmen to emphasize this instruction. (New York Times, 23 September 1990)

When the invasion went ahead Saddam's move was roundly condemned. Strangely, America's military were already prepared for a war against Saddam. While serving as Commander-in-Chief, United States Central Command, Norman Schwarzkopf pointed out that the army would have nothing to do if the Cold War with Russia was over. He worked overtime to throw out the old 'Zagros Mountains plan' which assumed a Soviet invasion and replaced it with 'Internal Look'. The new plan assumed an Iraqi invasion to seize Saudi oil fields. In late July 1990, Schwarzkopf staged a mock-up of 'Internal Look' just 2 weeks before Iraq invaded Kuwait. As he says himself, 'the movements of Iraq's real-world ground and air forces eerily paralleled the imaginary scenario in our game' – but then that was the point: the US planned and engineered the conflict from the start to the withdrawal of their troops, as an exercise in confidence-building and demonstrative performance of world power.[24]

President George H. W. Bush used the United Nations to rubber stamp a US-led coalition to defeat Saddam. Margaret Thatcher promised 'to send the 7th Armoured Brigade to the Gulf, comprising two armoured regiments with 120 tanks, a regiment of Field Artillery, a battalion of armoured infantry, anti-tank helicopters and all the necessary support'. 'It would be a completely self-supporting force, numbering up to 7,500.' Later she also sent:

> the 4th Brigade from Germany, comprising a regiment of Challenger tanks, two armoured infantry battalions and a regiment of Royal Artillery, with reconnaissance and supporting services. Together the two brigades would form the 1st Armoured Division. The total number of UK forces committed would amount to more than 30,000.[25]

Coalition forces dropped 88,500 tonnes of bombs in 109,000 sorties. In all 250,000 bombs were dropped, and only 22,000 of these were 'smart-bombs' (guided missiles). The bulk of the bombing was carried out by B52s flying at 40,000 feet. The death toll was around 180,000. British Prime Minister John Major was under pressure from some to pause the bombing, but not from Labour leader Neil Kinnock, who said, 'to be blunt, the best time to kick someone is when they are down'.[26]

Under Major-General Rupert Smith, Britain's 1st Armoured division took part in the attack on Iraqi forces retreating from Kuwait, the Battle of Norfolk, the biggest tank battle in the war, on 27 February 1991. British forces also took part in the attack on the retreating Iraqi forces on the Basra High Road on the same day. The Iraqis were bottled in when allied air forces attacked the roads out of Kuwait and destroyed them. Kill zones were assigned every 70 miles along the road. More than 2000 vehicles were destroyed and 25,000 killed. RAF Marshall David Craig said that the attack began to look 'more and more like butchery'.

Elsewhere, an RAF Tornado squadron leader 'who bombed a suspension bridge admitted that the bridge was in the centre of a populated area': 'Yes there will be civilian traffic,' the pilot said, 'but they could well be civilian contractors working on an airfield.'[27]

After inflicting a traumatic defeat on the Iraqi Army and the country, British Prime Minister John Major's proposal to create 'safe havens' from the air to stop attacks on the Kurdish minority laid the basis for RAF and USAF imposed 'no-fly zones'. As BBC correspondent Mohammed Darwish explained, there were 'continued air strikes in the south and north of the country where British and American planes are attacking under the disguise of patrolling the no-fly zones'. So, on 16 February 2001, British Tornado jets joined US F-15 aircraft bombing Baghdad on the claim that Iraqi forces were set to attack the RAF imposed 'no-fly zone' over northern Iraq.[28]

Iraq was subject to an embargo of food from September 1990 under the presciently numbered UN resolution 666. Sanctions remained in place with the modification that Iraq could – on condition it surrendered its oil exports to the UN – get food aid in return (while the UN deducted a percentage for costs). Denis Halliday, who managed the 'food for oil' programme, resigned in 1998, saying that he was 'overseeing the de-development and deindustrialisation of a modern country', and that 'sanctions are starving to death 6,000 Iraqi infants every month, ignoring the human rights of ordinary Iraqis'.[29]

The conclusion to the 1991 war also put Iraq under a 'weapons inspection' programme, where UN officials would examine military sites in Iraq to make sure that they had no 'weapons of mass destruction' (WMDs). The weapons inspection was wholly insincere, and there mainly to keep the issue of Iraqi WMDs in the public eye. Britain's MI6 had two clandestine programmes, 'Rockingham' and 'Mass Appeal', which were tasked with manipulating findings from the UN weapons inspection programme to manufacture evidence of WMDs even though the inspectorate's actual reports were that there were none – they had been destroyed in 1991. An official in Bill Clinton's administration explained that they counted on British military intelligence to help come up with the pretext for war: 'we were getting ready for action and we want the Brits to prepare'.[30]

The final decision to resume large-scale military operations against Iraq came in the wake of Osama bin Laden's Al Qaeda attack on the Twin Towers and the Pentagon on 11 September 2001. There was no connection between Osama bin Laden and Saddam Hussein other than that bin Laden had offered to take part in an Arab force *against* Iraq in 1991. Still, US President George W. Bush asserted that the perpetrators of 9/11 and Saddam Hussein were part of one continuous 'Axis of Evil' in his State of the Union address in January 2002. On 6 April 2002 Tony Blair met Bush and committed Britain to support a renewed all-out attack on Iraq.

On 19 February 2002 allied air forces flew 1700 sorties, 504 with cruise missiles in an attempt to 'shock and awe' Iraq. A total of 13,000 cluster bombs were dropped by the allies, 2170 by the UK. According to Human Rights Watch:

UK forces caused dozens of casualties when they used ground-launched cluster munitions in and around Basra. A trio of neighbourhoods in the southern part of the city was particularly hard hit. At noon on 23 March, a cluster strike hit Hay al-Munandissin al-Kubra (the engineers district) while Abbas Kadhim was throwing out the garbage. He had severe injuries to his bowel and liver, and a fragment that could not be removed from his heart.

Human Rights Watch went on to say that:

Three hours later, submunitions blanketed the neighbourhood

of Mishraq al-Jadid about two and a half kilometres north east. Iyad Jassim Ibrahim, a 26-year old carpenter, was sleeping in the front room of his house when shrapnel injuries caused him to lose consciousness. He later died in surgery. Ten relatives who were sleeping elsewhere in the house suffered shrapnel injuries. Across the street, the cluster strikes injured three children.[31]

In late March 2003 Britain's 7th Armoured Brigade fought Iraqi Army 51st Division for control of Basra. Around 500 Iraqis were killed in a tank battle fought by the Royal Scots Dragoon Guards. British losses were 11.

Between 25,000 and 50,000 Iraqis were killed in the initial invasion of Iraq. But that was by no means the end of the conflict in the country. Though the Iraqi Army was effectively defeated in 2003, under allied rule, the country was plunged into a destructive internecine conflict, as well as several rebellions against the allied occupation that cost hundreds of thousands of lives.

Britain supplied a force of 7200 to police Basra from 2003 to 2009. Hundreds of allegations of torture, assassination and ill-treatment have been laid against the British forces, leading to the setting up of a government Iraq Historic Allegations Team. British soldiers were dismayed to find they were to be held personally responsible and prosecuted for actions they had undertaken as part of military operations. A dossier of allegations passed on to the International Criminal Court brought matters to a head. In 2017 a British lawyer who had prepared some of the cases was struck off, accused of manufacturing evidence. Errors in the preparation of some cases were seized upon to undermine the IHAT, which has now been closed down.

Afghanistan: 2001-9

In 1980 the Soviet Union invaded Afghanistan and their forces were pinned down by fierce resistance from Afghan fighters – who were supported by American and British special services and \$40 billion in aid. Soviet withdrawal left the country in some turmoil, and the Islamist Taliban ('students') emerged as the dominant – and fiercely anti-western – force. Saudi Osama bin Laden was one of the 'Afghan Arabs' trained by the Pakistani secret services (the ISI) and his 'Al Qaeda' group planned the 9/11 attack on New York and the Pentagon from the country. In October 2001 American and British forces attacked the Taliban government in Afghanistan. Under Operation Enduring Freedom B-52 bombers, Lancers (and British cruise missiles) were sent to try to destroy Bin Laden's Tora Bora hide-out, followed by special forces, rangers and British marines.

Hamid Karzai was chosen as a western-friendly Pashtun at the Bonn Conference in December 2001, before being elected as interim president by tribal leaders the following year. Western strategists were hoping that the International Security Assistance Force could avoid alienating the local population as happened in Iraq – but with little success. The conflict has cost more than 100,000 Afghan lives, of whom two-thirds were Taliban fighters, and the rest government forces or civilians. Two thousand two hundred and seventy-one Americans have been killed in the fighting, and 456 British troops. The British operation within the ISAF is called Operation Herrick (2003-16). In the occupation and the prolonged (and ineffective) handover that followed, British forces were stationed in Helmand Province in the south west of the country between 2006 and 2009.

The British presence in Helmand lacked legitimacy. The British built Camp Bastion and sent troops to the main urban areas, the provincial capital Lashkar Gah (political HQ) and Musa Qala, Sangin, NawZad and Kajaki. As a force they were thinly stretched in an area the size of Wales.

When British forces handed over authority to local chiefs in Musa Qala, those same chiefs later asked the Taliban to enter the town peacefully, without a shot being fired. When the outside world got to hear about Britain's humiliation, the British Army had to stage an invasion of the town they had only recently abandoned, with a force of 4500 troops after the US Air Force bombed the town. British commander Major-General Graham Binns asked: 'If 90 per cent of the violence was directed against us, what would happen if we actually stepped back?'[32]

Later Afghan President Hamid Karzai protested that the British administration of Helmand Province had undermined the government's authority, ousting the local governor, and worse bribed Taliban militias to garner support. As international relations specialist David Chandler explains: 'The British policy of appeasing local opposition leaders, through buying their support and allowing the harvesting of opium poppies, has directly undermined the Afghan government.'[33]

British forces in Helmand were placed in arbitrary authority over people for whom they had no respect. Courts martial gave an insight into the day-to-day relationship. One soldier was found guilty of abusing an Afghan boy because he had pulled the boy's hand towards his crotch announcing to his fellow soldiers that the boy should 'touch my special place'. Another soldier admitted to having an Afghan man photographed with a sign which read 'silly Paki'.

British ambassador Sir Sherard Cowper-Coles wrote that the Afghan War gave the army *a raison d'être* it had lacked for years and resources on an unprecedented scale'. It is this, the unprecedented availability of resources, he says, that drove the strategy in Helmand and not an 'objective assessment of the needs of a proper counter-insurgency campaign in the province' – the point was just to keep the army busy. Since the British withdrawal from Helmand, Taliban forces have again contested the government for authority in Helmand and in 2017, 300 more US marines returned there.

Libya: 2011; Syria: 2018

Of all military interventions, the western coalition attack on Libya in 2011 is the most pointless. British, French and American leaders waged an air war on the government of Muammar Ghadaffi in Tripoli, in apparent support of rebel forces attacking the capital. British ships and aircraft fired Tomahawk missiles at Al Khums naval base and other targets. Defence analyst Mark Curtis explained that:

> British air strikes and cruise missile attacks began on 19 March and within the first month of what became a seven-month bombing campaign NATO had flown 2,800 sorties, destroying a third of Qadafi's military assets, according to NATO. The RAF eventually flew over 3,000 sorties over Libya, damaging or destroying 1,000 targets.[34]

The intervention did lead to the capture and killing of Ghadaffi, but the opposition government that replaced him had no authority and has struggled to fend off attacks by ISIS inspired militia ever since. As emerged later, the National Transitional Council, and the Libyan National Army that were recruited with British and American support, were substantially infiltrated by supporters of Islamic State. Conservative minister Alistair Burt conceded that the British security services had been meeting with 'former members of Libyan Islamic Fighting Group and 17 February Martyrs Brigade' in 2011. The allied attack was a show of strength, but one that only succeeded in undermining what plausible government existed in Libya and giving succour to militant Islamists.

Around the same time the US and British military were giving support to oppositionists challenging Syrian president Bashar al-Assad's regime. The Assad dictatorship was deeply unpopular and seemed a likely target for the kind of 'Arab Spring' protests to western analysts. Large protests were attacked by state forces leading to a situation close to civil war.

US and British special forces gave assistance to opposition militias, in particular the 'Free Syrian Army', which British military advisors helped to train in camps in Jordan. Britain also financed a public relations campaign for the oppositionists paying out £2.4 million. In 2012, the British military were claiming to be at the forefront of arming anti-Assad rebels, and helped President Obama's team to organise a 3000-ton arms airlift to opposition forces. However, as the leading Liberal Democrat Paddy Ashdown explained, those weapons were 'going almost exclusively to the more jihadist groups'.[35] In 2014 the Free Syrian Army joined with Islamic Front in an attempt to wrest control of Aleppo from Assad's forces.

In 2015 Russian forces joined the war on the side of the Assad regime, with air attacks that severely undermined the opposition, whether Islamist or moderate. Russian victories put pressure on the US-British policy in the region, and in 2018 after an alleged chemical attack by Syrian forces on the town of Douma, Britain, France and the US launched an air bombardment on government positions. Four Royal Air Force Tornado fighters and four Eurofighter Typhoon fighters fired Storm Shadow missiles at Syrian targets. The Royal Navy's air-defence destroyer HMS Duncan gave cover. In the bombardment the Barzah scientific research centre was severely damaged, along with two military bases. Just months before the Organisation for the Prohibition of Chemical Weapons had visited Barzah and declared that there were none there. The April 2018 airstrikes have been widely condemned since as gesture politics without any discernible strategic, let alone humanitarian, objective.

Endnotes

Introduction

1. Daily Record, 10 November 1914 https://www.dailyrecord. co.uk/opinion/sport/hotline/sports-hotline-live-shameful- celtic-4604153; Traynor, J. We Must Silence Spiteful Minority, Daily Record. 9 November 2009.; Carson, A. Celtic Fans in Poppy Outrage, The Scottish Sun. 7 November 2008.; Shame of Celtic after Fans Stage a Bloodstained Protest Against wearing Remembrance Day Poppies, 8 November 2010

2. Neil Faulkner, No Glory: The Real History of the First World War, Stop the War Coalition, p 22

Chapter One: Origins of the Red Poppy

1. For a more detailed explanation of Moina Michael and her campaign for the poppy's adoption as the memorial emblem, see Chapter Five of J.N. Saunders, The Poppy: A History of Conflict, Loss, Remembrance and Redemption

2. In the same place, p 106

3. The History of the Remembrance Poppy, Independent; http://www.independent.co.uk/life-style/history/the- history-of-the-remembrance-poppy-9852348.html

4. James Fox, Poppy Politics: Remembrance of Things Present; Cultural Heritage Ethics: Between Theory and Practice, OpenBook Publishers, p 1

5. Fox, Poppy Politics: Remembrance of Things Present; Cultural Heritage Ethics: Between Theory and Practice, OpenBook Publishers, p 1

6. For an example of the militant origins of the poem and its association with support for war, see Paul Fussell, The Great War and Modern Memory, Oxford; Oxford University Press, 1975, p 248-50

7. See John F. Prescott, In Flanders Fields: The Story of John

McCrae, The Boston Mills Press, 1985, p 67

8. John F. Prescott, In Flanders Fields: The Story of John McCrae, The Boston Mills Press, 1985, p 125, p 100, p 106, p 119

9. John F. Prescott, In Flanders Fields, p 128

10. John F. Prescott, In Flanders Fields, p 113

11. John F. Prescott, In Flanders Fields, p 135

12. N. J. Saunders, The Poppy: A History of Conflict, Loss, Remembrance and Redemption, 2014, p 99

13. James Fox, Poppy Politics: Remembrance of Things Present; Cultural Heritage Ethics: Between Theory and Practice, OpenBook Publishers, p 2

14. James Fox, Poppy Politics: Remembrance of Things Present; Cultural Heritage Ethics: Between Theory and Practice, OpenBook Publishers, p 2

Chapter Two: The Great War

1. John Harris, The Somme, Zenith, 1966, p 48

2. John Harris, The Somme, Zenith, 1966, p 108

3. This and what follows taken from Leon Trotsky's History of the Russian Revolution, London, Pluto Press, 1977

4. Times, 15 September 1916; Times, 12 August 1916

5. Neil Hanson, The Unknown Soldier, London, 2007, p 30, p 38

6. Dr Nicholas Butler quoted in Aldous Huxley, An Encyclopaedia of Pacifism, London, Chatto and Windus, 1937, p 32

7. Maurice Dobb, Trade Union Experience and Policy 1914-18, Lawrence and Wishart, 1940, p 19; Pierre Broué, The German Revolution 1917-1923, London, Merlin, 2006, p 59; Trotsky, Russian Revolution, London, Pluto, 1977, p 422

8. Adrian Gregory, The Last Great War, p 206

9. Kristian Coates-Ulrichsen, 'The Indian Army in Mesopotamia', in Rob Johnson, The British-Indian Army,

Cambridge Scholars, 2014, p 63; Hew Strachan, The First World War, 281

10. Pierre Broué, The German Revolution, p 92; Maurice Dobb, Trade Union Experience and Policy 1914-18, Lawrence and Wishart, 1940, p 18

11. Maurice Dobb, Trade Union Experience and Policy 1914-18, Lawrence and Wishart, 1940, p 20

12. Pierre Broué, The German Revolution 1917-1923, London, Merlin, 2006, p 59

13. Werner Abelshauser et al, BASF: The History of a Company, Cambridge UP, 2004, p 74

14. The Cumberland Miners' order was drawn from the Munitions of War Amendment Bill, see Hansard: HC Deb 04 January 1916 vol 77 cc877-81; William Paul, Hands off Russia, Glasgow, 1919, p 14

15. Maurice Dobb, Trade Union Experience and Policy 1914-18, Lawrence and Wishart, 1940, p 8

16. Lloyd George, Memoirs, Vol II, p 592-3

17. Hector Bolitho, Alfred Mond, 1933, p 200-1; Silvertown Explosion (Messrs. Brunner, Mond, and Company), Hansard, 28 May 1919

18. Francis Wood and Christopher Arnander, Betrayed Ally: China in the Great War, Pen and Sword Books, 2016

19. David Olusoga, The World's War, London, 2014, p 139, 143

20. Brock Millman, Managing Domestic Dissent in First Word War Britain, London, Frank Cass, 2000, p 40

21. Millman, p 80

22. Millman, p 81

23. Pierre Broué, The German Revolution 1917-1923, London, Merlin, 2006, p 51

24. Keith Middlemas, Politics in Industrial Society, London, 1979, p 119

25. Quoted in S. Pankhurst, The Home Front, London, 278

26. Pierre Broué, The German Revolution 1917-1923, London,

Merlin, 2006, p 59-60

27. Hew Strachan, The First World War, London, 2014, p 309
28. Leon Trotsky, History of the Russian Revolution, Pluto Press, 1977, p 1026 and Chapter 43
29. Hew Strachan, The First World War, p 280-2
30. This, and what follows, is taken from Pierre Broué's, The German Revolution 1917-1923, London, Merlin, 2006

Chapter Three: Why was there a War?

1. Norman Stone, World War One, 2009, p 23
2. This account taken from James Joll, The Origins of the First World War, Longman, 1992, especially p 24, 66
3. David Lloyd George, War Memoirs, 1938, pp 29-30
4. Fritz Fischer, Germany's Aims in the First World War, 1967, p 264
5. J. K. O'Connor, The Hun in Our Hinterland, Cape Town, 1914, p 8
6. Geoff Eley, 'Germany, the Fischer Controversy and the Context of War', in Anievas, Cataclysm 1914, Haymarket, Chicago, 2016, p 28; Rosa Luxemburg, 'Morocco', in Richard Day and Daniel Gaido (eds) Discovering Imperialism, Leiden, Brill, 2012, p 461
7. Diane Atkinson, Rise Up Women, Bloomsbury, 2018, p 370
8. Richard Shannon, The Crisis of Imperialism, Paladin, 1976, pp 358-9
9. Lord Salisbury quoted in Franklyn Johnson, Defence by Committee, Oxford University Press, 1960, p 11; Viscount Esher, The Committee of Imperial Defence, March, 1912, p 14
10. Robert Blyth et al, The Dreadnought and the Edwardian Age, National Maritime Museum, 2011, p 10
11. C. Stuart Linton, The Problem of Imperial Governance, London, 1912, p 119
12. William Paul, Hands off Russia, Glasgow, 1919, p 14

13. Robert Blyth et al, The Dreadnought and the Edwardian Age, National Maritime Museum, 2011, p 32

14. Karl Liebknecht, Militarism and Anti-Militarism, Rivers Press, 1973, p 49-50

15. T. G. Otte, 'Grey Ambassador', in Robert Blyth et al, The Dreadnought and the Edwardian Age, National Maritime Museum, 2011, p 68, p 64, p 67

16. William Manchester, The Arms of Krupp, 2003, p 271, p 275

17. William Manchester, The Arms of Krupp, 2003, p 280

18. This, and all the other reports on profits of UK companies in the foregoing, unless otherwise stated, are taken from the Manchester Guardian, editions of 31 May 1913, 28 May 1915; 25 February 1916, 28 May 1917, 11 June 1917; 21 June 1917, 19 April 1918, 5 March 1919

19. British expenditure, Josiah Stamp, Financial Aftermath of the War, London, Ernest Benn, 1932, p 41

20. Hector Bolitho, Alfred Mond, p 202

21. Keith Warren, Armstrongs of Elswick, Macmillan, 1989, p 189-90

22. Centenary of the Alkali Industry 1823-1923, United Alkali Company, 1923

23. Centenary of the Alkali Industry 1823-1923, United Alkali Company, 1923, p 8

24 Karl Liebknecht, Militarism and Anti-Militarism, Rivers Press, 1973, p 38

25. Werner Abelshauser, BASF: The History of a Company, Cambridge UP, 2004, p 157, p 173, pp 163-4

26. Werner Abelshauser, BASF: The History of a Company, Cambridge UP, 2004, p 165, p 171

27. William Manchester, The Arms of Krupp, 2003, p 311

28. Smedley Butler, War is a Racket, 1935, Chapter Two

29. Manchester Guardian, 13 March 1919

30. Excess Profits Duty, Association of the Chambers of Commerce, 24 April 1917, p 5, p 9, p 11, p 15

31. Manchester Guardian, 13 December 1919
32. Manchester Guardian, 18 March 1919; The Worker, 6 September 1919
33. Justin Marozzi, Baghdad, Penguin, 2015, p 273
34. George Antonius, The Arab Awakening, Libraire du Liban, Beirut, 1969, p 414, pp 170-1
35. Antonius, The Arab Awakening, pp 195-9, p 238
36. Antonius, The Arab Awakening, pp 244-50
37. Antonius, The Arab Awakening, pp 435
38. Antonius, The Arab Awakening, p 314
39. F. S. Northedge, The League of Nations, 1952, p 193
40. Fritz Fischer, Germany's Aims in the First World War, 1967, p 248
41. Robert Skidelsky, John Maynard Keynes: Hopes Betrayed 1883-1920, London, Macmillan, 1992, p 355; Mail on Sunday, 29 September 2010
42. The Worker, 10 November 1923
43. This and the foregoing in Werner Abelshauser, BASF: The History of a Company, Cambridge UP, 2004, pp 183-6
44. Young Plan at Work, Daily Worker, 11 November 1930

Chapter Four: Remembering the War Dead

1. The War Graves – The Question of Removals, Manchester Guardian, 29 November 1918; Philip Longworth, The Unending Vigil: A History of the Commonwealth War Graves Commission, 1967, p 58
2. Philip Longworth, The Unending Vigil, 1967, p 47
3. Richard van Emden, The Quick and the Dead, pp 275-6, p 253, p 255
4. See Neil Hanson, The Unknown Soldier, Random House, 2005, p 289
5. Richard van Emden, The Quick and the Dead, p 278
6. Manchester Guardian, 10 April 1919

7. Philip Longworth, The Unending Vigil: A History of the Commonwealth War Graves Commission, London, 1967, pp 56-7

8. David Olusoga, The World's War, p 144

9. Michele Barrett, Subalterns at War, (2007) Interventions: International Journal of Postcolonial Studies, 9:3, 451-74, p 455

10. Philip Longworth, The Unending Vigil: A History of the Commonwealth Graves Commission, 1917-67, p 120

11. Manchester Guardian, 12 November 1919

12. Richard van Emden, The Quick and the Dead, p 231, p 235

13. Manchester Guardian, 8 March 1919, The Tribunal, 21 November 1918

14. Manchester Guardian, 21 July 1919

15. Neil Hanson, The Unknown Soldier, 2007

16. The Worker, 19 July 1919

17. William Paul, Hands off Russia, Glasgow, 1919, p 15

18. Daily Mail edition of 12 November 1919

19. The Worker, 15 November 1919, and see Neil Hanson, The Unknown Soldier, 2007

20. Manchester Guardian, 12 November 1920

21. Manchester Guardian, 26 October 1920

22. Neil Hanson, The Unknown Soldier, 2007, p 349; Richard van Emden, The Quick and the Dead, p 133

23. Manchester Guardian, 12 November 1920; Neil Hanson, The Unknown Soldier, p 350; The Worker, 5 August 1922

24. The Worker, 5 August 1922

25. The Worker, 23 September 1922

26. Quoted in The Worker, 5 August, 1922

27. See report in NPC Circular, November-December 1924

28. The Worker, 10 November 1923

29. NPC Circular, October-November 1923

30. Manchester Guardian, 17 November 1923

31. NPC Circular, November-December 1924

32. Hansard HC Deb 23 May 1928 vol 217 cc1874-5; NPC News Bulletin, May 1928; NPC News Bulletin, June 1930
33. Quoted in Peace News, 14 November 1936
34. The Peace Review, November-December 1931
35. Peace News, 30 October 1937, Peace News, 6 November 1937
36. Peace News, 20 November 1937
37. Peace 6 November 1937; Peace News, 20 November 1937
38. Peace News, 10 November 1939
39. Daily Mail, 11 November 1941
40. The World Crisis, Volume II, 1915, p 276
41. L. P. Fox, The Truth About the ANZAC, Victorian Council Against War and Fascism, 1937 p 4
42. The Truth About the ANZAC, p 6
43. Communist Review, April 1939, p 240
44. Parliament of Australia, 28 April 1981, Page 1432; And see also the discussion at Evan Smith's Hatful of History blog, https://hatfulofhistory.wordpress.com/2014/04/25/anzac-day-and-protest-culture-in-australian-history/

Chapter Five: Ireland and the Poppy

1. The Blunt Instrument of War, Fintan O'Toole, Irish Times, Tuesday 31 July, 2007
2. General Sir Mike Jackson GC DSO ADC Gen, An Analysis of Military Operations in Northern Ireland: Operation Banner. Ministry of Defence, Army Code 71842, July 2006, Chapter 8, p 3, p 11
3. See Pat Finucane Centre report of Feile event: 'Speaking to the Enemy', 5 August 2015. See also http://veteransforpeace.org.uk/2014/the-wall-of-shame-by gus-hales/
4. The Blunt Instrument of War, Fintan O'Toole, Irish Times, Tuesday 31 July, 2007. See also Malachi O'Doherty, The Telling Year: Belfast 1972
5. Jude Collins, Carefully chosen victims from the conflict, www.judecollins.com/2018/05/carefully-chosen-victims-

conflict/

6. Edward Burke, An Army of Tribes: British Army Cohesion, Deviancy, and Murder in Northern Ireland, Liverpool University Press, 2018

7. Charles Townshend, Catholic Farmer's Killing in North and British army's tribal war, Irish Times, 31 March 2018 https://www.irishtimes.com/culture/books/catholic-farmer-s-killing-in-north-and-the-british-army-s-tribal-war-1.3442019

8. See Anne Cadwallader, Lethal Allies: British Collusion in Ireland, Mercier Press, 2013

9. Anne Cadwallader, Lethal Allies: British Collusion in Ireland

10. Is the poppy a tribute to closer British-Irish relations or a symbol with no place in Ireland?, Irish Post, 4 November 2015, https://www.irishpost.com/news/is-the-poppy-a-tribute-to-closer-british-irish-relations-or-a-symbol-with-no-place-in-ireland-71966

11. Owen Boycott, Ministry of Defence says sorry for killing of Majella O'Hare, Guardian, 28 March 2011, https://www.theguardian.com/uk/2011/mar/28/ministry-defence-apology-majella-ohare

12. Caraher family still seeking justice after 17 years, 10 January 2008, http://www.anphoblacht.com/contents/17986

13. See submission to the Forum for Peace and Reconciliation, Dublin Castle, April 1995. Retrieved 23 October 2015

14. Raymond Murray, State Violence: Northern Ireland, 1969-97, Mercier Press; Vincent Kearney, 'Aidan McAnespie: Soldier faces checkpoint killing charges,' BBC 19 June 2018 https://www.bbc.co.uk/news/uk-northern-ireland-44532887

15. West Brom match programme

16. See Michael Farrell, Northern Ireland: The Orange State, Pluto Press, 2nd revised edition, 1990

17. In November 1991 the co-author Kevin Rooney had to run

for his life after getting off the bus to see a gang of loyalist men waiting to check who was and who was not wearing a poppy, with several people who were not displaying the emblem receiving severe beatings

18. BBC insists presenters not required to wear poppy, Irish News, 29 October 2015
19. Queen's University Belfast: Ban on Poppy sale defeated. BBC N.I. News, 7 May 2014
20. Author Kevin Rooney grew up on the Ballymurphy housing estate
21. Irish News, 4 August 2007
22. See News Letter, Housing Executive: We did not fund UDA memorial plaque, Saturday, 2 August 2014
23. Chris Kilpatrick, How can we move on while memorials to terror keep appearing? Belfast Telegraph, 11 July 2014
24. The View, BBC Northern Ireland, 10 May 2018
25. Larisa Brown, Daily Mail, 12 May 2018
26. Kate Bellamy, As an Irish woman, I believe in wearing the remembrance poppy. Here's why…, The Journal, November 2013 http://www.thejournal.ie/readme/should-irish-people-wear-the-remembrance-poppy-1154189-Nov2013/
27. BBC News Website, 8 November 1917, http://www.bbc.co.uk/news/world-europe-41910166
28. Leo Varadkar's Shamrock-and-Poppy Badge Inspired By UVF Terror Symbol, ansionnachfionn.com, 8 November 2017
29. See Heartfield and Rooney, Who's Afraid of the Easter Rising? Zero Books, 2015, pp 5-6
30. See Philip Orr, The Road to the Somme: Men of the Ulster Division Tell Their Story, Black Staff Press, 1987 republished 2008; Brian Hanley, 'Look Back in Anger, Ireland and World War One', 27 October 2014, The Cedar Lounge Revolution, https://cedarlounge.wordpress.com/2014/10/27/look-back-in-anger-ireland-and-world-war-one/

31. See Poppy a 'valid recognition' of Irish soldiers in World Wars, Irish Times, Monday, 14 November 2005

32. Brian Hanley, 'Look Back in Anger, Ireland and World War One', 27 October 2014, The Cedar Lounge Revolution, https://cedarlounge.wordpress.com/2014/10/27/look-back-in-anger-ireland-and-world-war-one/

33. David McKitterick, Ireland's War of Independence: The chilling story of the Black and Tans, Independent 20 April 2006 https://www.independent.co.uk/news/world/europe/irelands-war-of-independence-the-chilling-story-of-the-black-and-tans-5336022.html

34. Belfast Telegraph, 30 October 2018

Chapter Six: A Century of British Militarism

1. Steven Balbirnie, Small War on a Violent Frontier: Colonial Warfare and British Intervention in Northern Russia, 1918-1919 in Small Nations and Colonial Peripheries in World War I, Gearóid Barr et al, eds, Brill, 2016 pp 194-7

2. Antony Lockley, Propaganda and the First Cold War in North Russia, 1918-1919, History Today, Vol. 53, No. 9 September 2003

3. Albert E Kahn and Michael M Sayers, The Great Conspiracy, Little, Brown and Company, Boston 1946

4. Evening Times, 6 September 1919

5. Richard Pipes, Russia under the Bolshevik Regime, New York, Alfred A. Knopf, 1994 p. 41

6. Lauri Kopisto, The British Intervention in South Russia 1918-1920, University of Helsinki, 2011, p 106

7. Lauri Kopisto, The British Intervention in South Russia 1918-1920, University of Helsinki, 2011, p 116, 121

8. 7 August 1918, Red Paper on Executions and Atrocities Committed in Russia, Peoples Russian Information Bureau, London, 1920

9. Martin Sixsmith, Russia, BBC Books, 2012, p 224, William

Paul, Hands off Russia, Glasgow, 1919, p 15

10. Diarmaid Ferriter, A Nation and Not a Rabble, p 86, p 205

11. Quoted in Shashi Tharoor, Inglorious Empire, Penguin, 2017, p 77, p 169, p 172

12. Jonathan Glancey, Guardian, 19 April 2003

13. Marek Pruszewicz, The 1920s British air bombing campaign in Iraq, BBC News, 7 October 2014 http://www.bbc.co.uk/news/magazine-29441383

14. UK troops admitted massacre, court told, Guardian, 9 May 2012

15. Mark Curtis, The Ambiguities of Power, Zed Books, 1995, pp 56-65

16. Mark Curtis, The Ambiguities of Power, 65-74

17. Mark Curtis, Ambiguities of Power, p 97

18. James Heartfield, Yemen: Taking another beating from the West, Spiked-online, 11 January 2010; and see the webpage Psyop of the Aden Emergency 1963-1967 by SGM Herbert A. Friedman (Ret.) https://www.psywar.org/aden.php

19. Jonathan Walker, Aden Insurgency: The Savage War in South Arabia 1962-67, Spellmount Ltd., Staplehurst, UK, 2005

20. The Battle of the Bogside, Living Marxism, August 1989

21. Fiona Fox, A Murder is not Announced, Living Marxism February 1991; Fiona Foster, The Peace of the Grave, Living Marxism, 1991; The Paranormal, Living Marxism, July 1992

22. Ben Brack, Living Marxism issue 71, September 1994

23. John Sweeney, Nato bombed Chinese deliberately, Observer, 17 October 1999

24. H Norman Schwarzkopf, It Doesn't Take a Hero, Bantam Press, 1992, p 292

25. Margaret Thatcher, The Downing Street Years, p 826, p 828

26. John Major, Autobiography, Harper Collins, 1999, p 236

27. Mark Curtis, Ambiguities of Power, p 190, p 192

28. Rageh Omar, Revolution Day, Viking, 2004, p 73; Guardian, 19 February 2001

29. Rageh Omar, Revolution Day, p 36
30. Mark Curtis, Unpeople, London, Vintage, 2004, pp 48-9
31. Quoted in Mark Curtis, Unpeople, pp 16-17
32. David Chandler, Britain's theatrical war against the Taliban, spiked-online.com, 11 December 2007
33. Britain's key weapon in Afghanistan: the bribe, Spiked-online.com, 3 January 2008
34. Mark Curtis, Overthrowing Qadafi in Libya: Britain's Islamist Boots on the Ground, 30 August 2016, markcurtis. info/2016/08/30/overthrowing-qadafi-in-libya-britains-islamist-boots-on-the-ground/
35. Mark Curtis, How Britain engaged in a covert operation to overthrow Assad, 26 April, 2018 http://markcurtis. info/2018/04/26/how-britain-engaged-in-a-covert-operation-to-overthrow-assad/

Index

CULTURE, SOCIETY & POLITICS

Contemporary culture has eliminated the concept and public
figure of the intellectual. A cretinous anti-intellectualism
presides, cheer-led by hacks in the pay of multinational
corporations who reassure their bored readers that there is
no need to rouse themselves from their stupor. Zer0 Books
knows that another kind of discourse – intellectual without
being academic, popular without being populist – is not only
possible: it is already flourishing. Zer0 is convinced that in
the unthinking, blandly consensual culture in which we live,
critical and engaged theoretical reflection is more important
than ever before.
If you have enjoyed this book, why not tell other readers by
posting a review on your preferred book site.

Recent bestsellers from Zero Books are:

In the Dust of This Planet
Horror of Philosophy vol. 1
Eugene Thacker
In the first of a series of three books on the Horror of
Philosophy, *In the Dust of This Planet* offers the genre of horror
as a way of thinking about the unthinkable.
Paperback: 978-1-84694-676-9 ebook: 978-1-78099-010-1

Capitalist Realism
Is there no alternative?
Mark Fisher
An analysis of the ways in which capitalism has presented itself
as the only realistic political-economic system.
Paperback: 978-1-84694-317-1 ebook: 978-1-78099-734-6

Rebel Rebel
Chris O'Leary
David Bowie: every single song. Everything you want to know,
everything you didn't know.
Paperback: 978-1-78099-244-0 ebook: 978-1-78099-713-1

Cartographies of the Absolute
Alberto Toscano, Jeff Kinkle
An aesthetics of the economy for the twenty-first century.
Paperback: 978-1-78099-275-4 ebook: 978-1-78279-973-3

Malign Velocities
Accelerationism and Capitalism
Benjamin Noys
Long listed for the Bread and Roses Prize 2015, *Malign
Velocities* argues against the need for speed, tracking
acceleration as the symptom of the ongoing crises of capitalism.
Paperback: 978-1-78279-300-7 ebook: 978-1-78279-299-4

Meat Market
Female Flesh under Capitalism
Laurie Penny
A feminist dissection of women's bodies as the fleshy fulcrum
of capitalist cannibalism, whereby women are both consumers
and consumed.
Paperback: 978-1-84694-521-2 ebook: 978-1-84694-782-7

Poor but Sexy
Culture Clashes in Europe East and West
Agata Pyzik
How the East stayed East and the West stayed West.
Paperback: 978-1-78099-394-2 ebook: 978-1-78099-395-9

Romeo and Juliet in Palestine
Teaching Under Occupation
Tom Sperlinger
Life in the West Bank, the nature of pedagogy and the role of a
university under occupation.
Paperback: 978-1-78279-637-4 ebook: 978-1-78279-636-7

Sweetening the Pill
or How we Got Hooked on Hormonal Birth Control
Holly Grigg-Spall
Has contraception liberated or oppressed women? *Sweetening the Pill* breaks the silence on the dark side of hormonal contraception.
Paperback: 978-1-78099-607-3 ebook: 978-1-78099-608-0

Why Are We The Good Guys?
Reclaiming your Mind from the Delusions of Propaganda
David Cromwell
A provocative challenge to the standard ideology that Western power is a benevolent force in the world.
Paperback: 978-1-78099-365-2 ebook: 978-1-78099-366-9

Readers of ebooks can buy or view any of these bestsellers by clicking on the live link in the title. Most titles are published in paperback and as an ebook. Paperbacks are available in traditional bookshops. Both print and ebook formats are available online.

Find more titles and sign up to our readers' newsletter at http://www.johnhuntpublishing.com/culture-and-politics

Follow us on Facebook
at https://www.facebook.com/ZeroBooks

and Twitter at https://twitter.com/Zer0Books